SEEK
HIM
VOLUME 1

SEEK HIM VOLUME I

Testing Your Spiritual Comfort Zone

NATASHA L. FOREMAN

DOME Life Publishing

Copyright @ 2020 by Natasha L. Foreman
D.O.M.E. Life Publishing
Foreman & Associates, LLC
Post Office Box 1912, Mableton, GA 30126

First Edition, 2020
Cover Artwork Image: ID 94257545
@ Publicdomainphotos - Dreamstime.com

Author Image: Laquanda Bruce, Taken by LaLa Photography
lalaphotography.com

All rights reserved. No part of this book may be reproduced in any manner whatsoever without written permission except in the case of brief quotations embodied in critical articles and reviews.

D.O.M.E. Life Publishing, Imprint of Foreman & Associates, LLC
Books may be purchased in bulk for educational, business, fundraising, or sales promotional use.
For information, please email info@DomeLifePublishing.com.

Library of Congress Control Number: 2020916673
ISBN 13: 978-1-7355450-0-4 [paperback]
ISBN 13: 978-1-7355450-1-1 [e-book]
Printed in the United States of America

Scripture quotations marked (AMP) are taken from the Amplified Bible, Copyright © 1954, 1958, 1962, 1964, 1965, 1987 by The Lockman Foundation. Used by permission. Scripture quotations marked (ASV) are taken from the American Standard Version, published in 1901 by Thomas Nelson & Sons; public domain.

Scripture quotations marked (CEV) are taken from the CONTEMPORARY ENGLISH VERSION, Copyright© 1995 by the American Bible Society. Used by permission. Scripture quotations marked (CSB) have been taken from the Christian Standard Bible®, Copyright © 2017 by Holman Bible Publishers. Used by permission. Christian Standard Bible® and CSB® are federally registered trademarks of Holman Bible Publishers. Scripture quotations marked (CJB) are taken from the COMPLETE JEWISH BIBLE, Copyright© 1998 by David H. Stern. Published by Jewish New Testament Publications, Inc. www.messianicjewish.net. Distributed by Messianic Jewish Resources Int'l. www.messianicjewish.net. All rights reserved. Used by permission. Scripture quotations marked (Dar) are taken from the DARBY BIBLE, published in 1867, 1872, 1884, 1890; public domain. Scripture quotations marked (DRC1752) are taken from the Douay-Rheims Challoner Revision, public domain. Edited by Richard Challoner, 1749-1752, translated by English College at Douai and Rheims. Scripture quotations marked ESV are from the ESV® Bible (The Holy Bible, English Standard Version®), copyright © 2001 by Crossway Bibles, a publishing ministry of Good News Publishers. Used by permission. All rights reserved. Scripture quotations marked HCSB are been taken from the Holman Christian Standard Bible®, Copyright © 1999, 2000, 2002, 2003 by Holman Bible Publishers. Used by permission. Holman Christian Standard Bible®, Holman CSB®, and HCSB® are federally registered trademarks of Holman Bible Publishers. KJV: King James Version Used by Public Domain worldwide with the exception of the United Kingdom. In that regard: Scripture quotations from The Authorized (King James) Version. Rights in the Authorized Version in the United Kingdom are vested in the Crown. Reproduced by permission of the Crown's patentee, Cambridge University Press. Scripture taken from The Message. Copyright Â© 1993, 1994, 1995, 1996, 2000, 2001, 2002. Used by permission of NavPress Publishing Group. Scripture quotations taken from the New American Standard Bible® (NASB), Copyright © 1960, 1962, 1963, 1968, 1971, 1972, 1973, 1975, 1977, 1995 by The Lockman Foundation. Used by permission. www.Lockman.org. Scripture quotations marked (NIV) are taken from the Holy Bible, New International Version®, NIV®. Copyright © 1973, 1978, 1984, 2011 by Biblica, Inc.™ Used by permission of Zondervan. All rights reserved worldwide. www.zondervan.com The "NIV" and "New International Version" are trademarks registered in the United States Patent and Trademark Office by Biblica, Inc.™ Scripture taken from the New King James Version®. Copyright © 1982 by Thomas Nelson. Used by permission. All rights reserved.

Scripture quotations marked (NLT) are taken from the Holy Bible, New Living Translation, copyright ©1996, 2004, 2015 by Tyndale House Foundation. Used by permission of Tyndale House Publishers, a Division of Tyndale House Ministries, Carol Stream, Illinois 60188. All rights reserved. Scripture taken from The Orthodox Jewish Bible Copyright © 2011 by AFI International. All rights reserved.

I dedicate this book to my parents, Gwendolyn
Foreman and the late Robert E. Foreman, Jr.
Thank you for always loving, encouraging,
inspiring, and supporting me.
To my sister Alexandra and my nephew Logan,
here's to big dreams that turn into awesome
opportunities and experiences.
Also, to each person that reads this
book—through seeking God, may
you find, embrace, and live your truth!

Guiding Scripture

Trust in the Lord with all thine heart; and lean not unto thine own understanding.

—PROVERBS 3:5-6 KJV

Trust in ADONAI with all your heart; do not rely on your own understanding. In all your ways acknowledge him; then he will level your paths.

— MISHLEI (PROVERBS) 3:5-6 CJB

Trust in Hashem with all thine lev, and lean not unto thine own binah. In all thy drakhim acknowledge Him, and He shall make yosher thy orkhot.

— MISHLE (PROVERBS) 3:5-6 OJB

Contents

Acknowledgement — xix
Welcome Prayer — xxi
Introduction — xxiii
Getting The Most From This Book — xxvii

MONTH ONE
FIRST STEPS

PONDER THIS: Month 1	2
Day 1: Virtuosity	3
Day 2: Be The Tree	8
Day 3: Release Yourself to God	12
Day 4: He is All	14
Day 5: Your Gifts and Talents	16
Day 6: Believing and Trusting Jesus	19
Day 7: How Are You Investing Your Time?	23
Day 8: Jesus IS Our Proof	25
Day 9: Love is the Perfect Bond of Unity	28
Day 10: Protecting Your Heart	31
Day 11: God's Compassion	34

Day 12: Anticipation	36
Day 13: Standing Tall in Your Conviction	38
Day 14: Running God's Race, Not Man's	41
Day 15: Pray For The Stubborn	43
Day 16: Believing in God	46
Day 17: God Rescues	49
Day 18: Wisdom	51
Day 19: Patience	53
Day 20: God's Command	55
Day 21: Glorify God	57
Day 22: Learning From Our Elders	59
Day 23: Waiting for God	61
Day 24: The Answers Are Inside of You	63
Day 25: God's Faithfulness	65
Day 26: Let the Storm Pass	67
Day 27: Pain	69
Day 28: What the Lord Requires of You	71
Day 29: God's Protection	75
Day 30: Grace	79
Day 31: Caring For Your Temple	81
GO BEYOND: Month 1	84

MONTH TWO
LOOK WITHIN

PONDER THIS: Month 2	90

Day 32: Forgiveness	91
Day 33: God's Will	94
Day 34: Stare Down Your Mountains	96
Day 35: Putting God First	99
Day 36: Celebrate Life	101
Day 37: Elders Are Pillars	103
Day 38: Stop Resisting	105
Day 39: Fear	108
Day 40: Servant Leaders vs. Self-Serving	110
Day 41: Recklessness	112
Day 42: Watch Your Words	114
Day 43: Testify to God's Greatness	118
Day 44: Our Choices	120
Day 45: Nobody Has Your Back Like God Does	123
Day 46: LOVE	125
Day 47: Free From The Law of Sin & Death	127
Day 48: God's Provisions	130
Day 49: God is Always Working	133
Day 50: Will You Reject God?	136
Day 51: Grace of God... Seek Him in Everything	138
Day 52: Your Heart	140
Day 53: There is No Hiding The Truth	142
Day 54: Getting Aligned	146
Day 55: God and Jesus Have You	148

Day 56: Wait For Your Harvest — 151
Day 57: Be On Your Guard — 154
Day 58: What You Give, You Get — 157
Day 59: Faith — 160
Day 60: Letting Go Of Your Past — 162
Day 61: God Hears Us, Even In Our Silence — 164
Day 62: Being Prepared For Your Blessings — 167
GO BEYOND: Month 2 — 169

MONTH THREE
WHAT DO YOU SEE?

PONDER THIS: Month 3 — 172
Day 63: Know Your Truth...You're Already Equipped — 173
Day 64: God's Gift is Within You — 176
Day 65: Your Life Reflects Your Relationship With God — 178
Day 66: How Deep and Great is Your Love? — 181
Day 67: What Have You Been Called to Do? — 184
Day 68: The Seed and The Sower — 188
Day 69: See Deeper — 191
Day 70: Be True to Your Word — 193
Day 71: Your Plans May Not Be God's Plans — 196
Day 72: What You Seek, You Will Find — 199
Day 73: Finish What You Start — 202
Day 74: Leave Your Worries Behind... — 205
Day 75: The Enemy is About Smoke and Mirrors — 207

Day 76: Check Yourself Before You Wreck Yourself	211
Day 77: Want to Make God Laugh? Tell Him Your Plans	213
Day 78: Be in Alignment	216
Day 79: We Have All Sinned	218
Day 80: Because of Your Faith, Some Will Plot	221
Day 81: His Grace is Upon You	224
Day 82: Value Every Experience Through Gratitude	226
Day 83: Peace	228
Day 84: Your Pride and Ego Will Make You a Fool	230
Day 85: Even Through Fear, Jesus Pressed Forward	234
Day 86: Relying Upon God	236
Day 87: Worship God Not Man	238
Day 88: It's Thanksgiving	240
Day 89: Don't Be Confined to One Book	242
Day 90: Silence The Naysayers	244
Day 91: Tell The Enemy to Get Out of Your Way	246
Day 92: Get Rest, But Don't Be Lazy	248
Day 93: Soldier For Christ	250
GO BEYOND: Month 3	253
MONTH FOUR: WHAT DO YOU FEEL?	255
PONDER THIS: Month 4	256
Day 94: Time Is As Precious As You Make It	257
Day 95: You Are Saved By The Gospel	259

Day 96: Jealousy is Like Cancer	261
Day 97: Abundance Through Obedience	264
Day 98: Repent	267
Day 99: Stretch Out of Your Comfort Zone	269
Day 100: Look Inside	272
Day 101: Do Your Part	274
Day 102: Let Go of the Reigns	276
Day 103: Seeking Guiding Wisdom From Advisors	279
Day 104: "Closet" Christians	282
Day 105: Are You a Dreamer?	287
Day 106: God Is Not Mocked. What You Sow, You Reap.	290
Day 107: You Can't Fool God	294
Day 108: Keep Your Armor and Shield Close	297
Day 109: Smile	299
Day 110: Righteousness	301
Day 111: The Invited	304
Day 112: Leasing From God	306
Day 113: God Opens Our Eyes to Infinite Possibilities	310
Day 114: Stop Comparing	313
Day 115: Removing Blinders	316
Day 116: His Voice	319
Day 117: Riding Through Storms	321
Day 118: You Don't Receive More or Less of His Love	324
Day 119: Your Commitment	326

Day 120: Inner Turmoil	330
Day 121: Be on Guard	332
Day 122: We're Never Sure How We're Being Used	335
Day 123: Just Share Your Story	337
Day 124: It's Not You, It's Him	339
GO BEYOND: Month 4	341

NEXT STEPS

Consider This: Month 1	344
Consider This: Month 2	345
Consider This: Month 3	346
Consider This: Month 4	350
Conclusion	353
NOTES	355
MORE THANK YOU'S	357
About the Author	361

Acknowledgement

Let me first start by thanking my Creator, my heavenly Father-Mother. Without Elohim ["God" in Hebrew], this book would not be possible. This has been a multi-year journey guided by His loving push, correction, and realignment. He has brought some amazing people into my life that have helped me to pour my all into this body of work. I pray that it brings more people to Him. I give Him all the glory! I'm grateful for the support and encouragement that I've received over the years from family, friends, and associates. I contemplated what this book would be. There have been several revisions made since I typed the first word. In the end, I am pleased. I would like to thank my family for their love and support. Thank you for your wisdom and guidance. I pray to always honor you through my daily walk.

I would like to thank my mom for providing me with amazing feedback and suggestions for this book. Mom even helped me with enhancing the Speak Your Truth section. Thank you again, mom. Thank you for the daily prayers and motivations. Thank you for always trying to find the silver lining in every cloud. I used to tease you about it. Now I see how God works in and through you. Never stop letting Him pour into you. I love and appreciate you. To my sister, Alexandra, I am grateful that God blessed me with you. Thank you for loving and supporting me through this book journey. I pray that some version of this book helps you in whatever ways that you and God are working on. May it inspire and encourage you as a woman, servant, and mother to my amazing nephew Logan. May he grow up with this and other books his auntie writes, knowing who he is and to Whom he belongs. I love you Poonka and Snookums!

Special thanks to my aunt Debborah for encouraging me to speak my truth, find myself, and be myself. And thank you for encouraging me to live each day moment by moment. Thank you for knowing and seeing me. You don't know how much our conversations helped to shape this book and the two that follow. To my aunt Valerie, I appreciate you for your encouragement over the years. I also want to thank you for your feedback and contributions to my Breaking Bread With Natasha blog. Thank you for your feedback on this book and for suggesting that I open the book with a prayer, to bless all that read it. I claim the vision that you have for this and future books. Thank you for the prayers.

Arleen Hayes, thank you for your feedback and encouragement. I'm glad that my book has excited and inspired you. Your daily inspirational text messages have helped me through some of the roughest of days. You will always be my sister-in-love and I will always love you.

Thank you, Kerric Bennett. You encouraged, challenged, and pushed me. You inspired, questioned, and supported me and my efforts with this book. You called me out when I wasn't digging deep enough. You challenged me to ask questions and go beyond my comfort zone. Our countless conversations helped to shape and inspire sections of this book. Thank you for your help on How to Use This Book, as well as the Ponder This, Consider This sections. Even as I type these words, you still let me come to you and consume hours of your day, sharing with you how God inspired or led me to further research that I can use on future projects. Thank you. I'm truly grateful.

Judy Bennett, thank you for your loving support. Your feedback on my book brought me to tears. It inspires and encourages me to share this book with as many people as I can. Milton Little, thank you for reading and providing feedback on the book. Thank you for being a true friend. I appreciate you in ways that words can't describe. Frederick Jones, thank you for your feedback and for asking the big question, "So how's your book coming along Natasha?" every few months.

Welcome Prayer

Special thank you to my aunt Valerie who suggested that I share a prayer, to help set the coordinates for this chartered course:

Father, I pray that You guide me and those who read this book to a better understanding of our purpose; to have a better, stronger, more authentic relationship with You. Guide us to see our roles as stewards, ambassadors, servants, rays of Your Light, truth seekers and truth speakers, living fully in our truth. Guide us past the rhetoric, close-minded, false narratives that have served no one but our egos and the enemy. Help us in and through our exploration so that our hearts may be warmed, opened and receptive to all of Your children—not just those we prefer.

Guide us to see the reality of having dominion over our own unique experiences, so that we may shatter stereotypes and other barriers that keep us from fully expressing and demonstrating our oneness with You. We are You and You are us. We are one. Guard us from the limits that we place upon ourselves and others. Let us see beyond age, gender, race, color, religion, nationality, ability, and sexual orientation. For You are all-encompassing, so the fragments that we obsess over are only mere pieces of You that we sadly neglect, exploit, and abuse. Free our minds and hearts from the shackles of ignorance and fear, so that we can one day free our bodies from this bondage. May we fully embrace who and what we are, in all ways, and without limits.

Love is supposed to be the religion. Love is the ultimate religion. Love is the way to You. Love is You and You are love. That means, as Your children, Your creations, we are to love fully and without restrictions. Help us to educate and empower ourselves so that we can put down the weapons of mass destruction that keep us disconnected from You. Then we can open our arms to embrace each other, see each other, and love each other as You love us. I say these words with the belief that the Bible is a compilation of bodies of work, written by people to express, outline, highlight, testify, and make clear their love for You and Your love, promise to, and desire for all of Your children. Thank You for helping me to use it to shape this body of work and challenge everything that I thought I knew.

Thank You for all of the people that You used in the past and those that You use now to reach us and teach us, at the levels where we were, are, and will be. Thank You for Your love, patience, and grace. I give You all of the glory. Amen.

Introduction

It's kind of funny that I wrote this book. Let me clarify that statement. I was one of "those" Christians who steered clear of speaking about religion. I kept my religious and spiritual beliefs, private. I always took the position that "people fight and kill over religion and politics". So I chose to remain on neutral ground when either topic jumped into a conversation. I felt comfortable being a "closet" Christian. For several years I struggled with religion and religious people. I steered clear of a church unless I attended one of my grandmothers' churches. Then God stepped in, used some amazing people to encourage me, and He guided me to share the conversations (prayers) that I have with Him on my blog, Breaking Bread With Natasha, and then seven years later—in August 2016 I began planning this book.

It was a rocky start at first because I didn't have a true understanding of the purpose of the book, so my passion waned. Several weeks later I stopped typing. I picked back up in 2017 while going through my divorce. That was a very trying time to write words of courage, strength, grace, forgiveness, healing, and love—especially when I was in so much pain. It wasn't until 2018 that I stepped back and actually prayed about the purpose of this book. Then things began making sense. I started to see the ways this book would help me in the next phase of my spiritual journey. As I started rearranging my book, things started to click and make sense. My book started to flow.

When 2019 rolled in I finally felt a growing excitement for what was developing. I'm grateful to Kerric Bennett for helping me to begin push past my comfort zone. He knew that I didn't want to write for the sake of writing. It has helped me to challenge everything that I've learned. I now take into consideration the historical and cultural perspectives. For me, this stage of my journey has been a look back into a mirror of my life. I need to acknowledge the things that I haven't addressed, rectified, and healed from. It has also enhanced my testimony and reshaped my view of myself.

I am no longer limited by the title of Christian. I am a child of God and follower of Yeshua ("Jesus") whom He sent to show us the way. God has been guiding me through past and current trials. This has encouraged me to give my best effort—to pour myself into this book and the ones that follow. The goal has been to create what I've been looking for in a spiritual guidebook and study tool. I'm confident that I accomplished this. I hope that this book inspires and challenges me. I hope it does the same for you. Before I escort you to the Getting The Most From This Book section, let me share some things that should be beneficial for some of you.

What This Book Is Not

This book is not to shame, guilt-trip, bully, or pressure you to conform, convert, think, or believe a certain way. This book is not designed to manipulate you into thinking, speaking, or behaving in one way or another. There is no right way to be a Christian or any other religious title that you want to give yourself. There is no specific way to pray to, love, praise, or glorify God. You and God have a unique relationship and it may look totally different than His relationship with others. This book is for you to seek, discover, know, embrace, speak, and live your truth. In whatever way, it comes to you. This is your step in testing your comfort zone so that you can push past it.

Interchanging of Names

You will see that I may call God by different names, like Father, Elohim, Father-Mother, Lord, and Creator. I always attempt to make it clear that I am referring to Him and no one else, as the Bible's many authors alternated words that have confused many of us from time to time. In the Old Testament, Lord in one respect could mean God and in the New Testament, it could mean Jesus. You will also see that I sometimes call Jesus my savior, or by his Hebrew name Yeshua. I may interchange these words, but mostly, you will see my use of Jesus, because it is what most English speakers were taught to call him. Please read the **Greater Context** section inside of **Seek Him: Workbook 1**, for further clarification on this and other relevant points.

Humor

From time to time, you will notice that I use humor to make a point or to express my thoughts or feelings. It's not contrived, it's my personality. I understand that for some people this can be unsettling. You learned that religion is serious and we shouldn't use humor in that context. In response, I remind you that God is the Creator of joy, laughter, and humor, and He intended for us to use them freely. Also, Jesus used humor to make serious points. Read Luke 12:16-21 and Matthew 7:3-5, as two examples. Did you not laugh when you read that Jesus said it would be easier to thread a camel through the eye of a needle than for rich people to get into heaven [Luke 18:24-25]. If you can't see the sarcastic humor in those statements then you may need to spend some time with a child. They get it. Lighten up. Allow God's gift of humor to help you through the rough, awkward, sensitive, and the unknown.
*Note: "Camel" is actually the word "rope" in Aramaic. Greek translation did not understand the context of this.

Getting The Most From This Book

This book is divided into four months. Each month represents our journey towards living on and in our purpose. I'm not saying that by the time you finish reading this book or even the entire series, that you will know, embrace, and live your truth. But through daily seeking and walking with God, we grow better. We're all at different stages in our growth. Some of us (like myself) are having to re-learn lessons until we are ready for the next steps. When we see and think about these stages of our development, we can push ourselves, to go deeper into our studies. We can go farther through our service or in our relationship with self and God.

This book has 124 daily messages. Each month starts with "trivia". Each day has a theme, one or more Bible verses, a reflection, prayer, and an activity. At the end of each month, a more extensive activity is presented to encourage and challenge you.

Ponder This, Consider This

This is the monthly trivia that I just mentioned. Both sections present commentary, scenarios, statements, phrases, and more from the Bible—as well as from sources that we assume came from the Bible. The month begins with **Ponder This**. Then you are encouraged to visit the

Consider This chapter (towards the end of the book), to read revealed truths, clarifying details, and facts supported by customs, religion, and history. The Apostle Paul wrote in 1 Thessalonians 5:21, "*But examine everything carefully; hold fast to that which is good...*" and taking that to heart, I challenge myself and you to examine everything carefully. Strive to determine if a source is truthful and right before you recite something or someone. That is what Ponder This and Consider This allows us to do. They will further enhance your journey towards your truth!

Reflection & Prayer

After reading the Bible verse we reflect on the message. It's the things that you and I may question, wonder, ponder, desire, or struggle with. Following the reflection is a prayer. This section can be an added benefit if you struggle with or feel uncomfortable praying. For years I struggled with praying because I thought there was a formal or special kind of way to speak to God. The truth is the only right way to pray is your way. Do what feels comfortable to you, what is natural to you when you sit back and begin to speak. God is listening, He's not concerned about the formalities. He's concerned about His relationship with you.

Speak Your Truth

Speak Your Truth consists of eight statements or affirmations that came to me in a vision, after reading about an affirmation book. Speak Your Truth serves as a space to share. You can write about your feelings, self-perception, beliefs, what you're grateful for, and what you're committed to for the day. Thanks to my mom for suggesting that I include the statements "I will improve" and "I am proud of myself because". There is a little child within us that is sometimes fearful. The words that we speak can either empower or hinder that child. Our affirmations are also our declarations to God. While we study the Bible and pray to God, each day you can also Speak Your Truth.

Notes

I hope you have adequate space to take notes. There are also large sections in the workbook.

Go Beyond

After each month, you are encouraged to take your journey deeper. Some of the activities challenge you to put into practice what you may have been seeing as a theory. Or put another way, walking the walk. It is one thing for us to talk about Jesus, the prophets, love, forgiveness, grace, and humility. Demonstrating the qualities of God makes our alignment with Him more plausible. You must devote some time to complete this leg on the journey. Don't skip over it, don't rush through it. You are investing time in your relationship with God and self. Be intentional when beginning and completing the work as outlined. Make it yours. Make it personal. It's your life, your journey. If you want more you must give more. You need to Go Beyond.

Seek Him: The Workbook

Throughout this book, you will see references to this workbook. You will also be directed to read the **Go Deeper** and **Greater Context** sections of the workbook. The **Go Deeper** section should be attempted immediately after completing the **Speak Your Truth** section at the end of each week. It is a deeper exploration of the Bible, shared more simply. The **Greater Context** section found in the workbook provides historical, cultural, and other insights to give you a better perspective.

Bible Translations

This book uses 16 Bible translations. Why? There are limitations with translations. The Bible had more than 11,000 Hebrew, Greek, and Aramaic words. Most English translations use roughly 6,000 words, each with their own 'slant' on meaning. Which may be ignored by readers unless you compare the translations. Reason two, we grow to think that we know verses because we have them committed to memory. Unfortunately, we confuse our translation to be the only one, the right one.

Let me give you an example. Recite the Lord's Prayer. There are several versions. Luke 11:2-4 ESV has a version. Mark 6:9-13 (NIV) has yet another version. Words have meaning. If you think that you already know a verse because you can recite it, then you risk missing the full meaning.

That's All Folks

Well, that's that. I hope that I've described in great enough detail how to use this book and the purpose of the sections and that I've made clear the various ways that you can use them and the other features mentioned. This is your life and your journey. I hope that by addressing the things that I desire most in a book, I've also spoken to and addressed the needs of some of you. Even if it's only one person. Enjoy the book, lessons, activities, challenges, and speaking your truth. I hope that you go deeper and then go beyond. There are no limits when God is in it, so boldly take the next step!
God bless you,
Natasha

MONTH ONE

First Steps

---

*Let us search and test derakheinu (our ways),
and let us turn again to Hashem.*

—EKHAH 3:40 OJB

[LAMENTATIONS 3:40 KJV]

Take your first steps to your fresh start...

PONDER THIS: Month 1

We are said to be spiritual beings[1] in human form. In ancient, and in some modern cultures, a child is given a name based on certain conditions and factors. It could be in obedience to prophecy, maternal visions, a name given by God, or based on physical factors like weather, seasons, temperament or complexion of the baby, and more.

It is both stated and implied that Jesus was of the lineage of David. Jesus being a descendant of the children of Israel means that he has Jewish-Palestinian heritage and hence spoke Aramaic. Millions argue whether Jesus was always a deity, later became one, or was crucified simply as a man. But, if we hold on to the belief that we are all spiritual beings, that means Jesus was and is a spiritual being.

The name Jesus is not Hebrew, Aramaic, Jewish, Palestinian, or the like. So, is Jesus his birth name, given name, or nickname? If none of the above, then who is Jesus? Who are we praying to and about? What spirit are we calling out to each day? Write your thoughts below.

At some point this month, please journey to the **Consider This: Month 1** section located towards the end of the book. Let's see if your thoughts align with historical and cultural facts.

Day 1: Virtuosity

The Virtuous Woman Celebrated

"Who can find a virtuous and capable wife? She is more precious than rubies. Her husband can trust her, and she will greatly enrich his life. She brings him good, not harm, all the days of her life... She goes to inspect a field and buys it; with her earnings she plants a vineyard. She is energetic and strong, a hard worker...She extends a helping hand to the poor and opens her arms to the needy...She is clothed with strength and dignity, and she laughs without fear of the future. When she speaks, her words are wise, and she gives instructions with kindness...Her children stand and bless her. Her husband praises her: "There are many virtuous and capable women in the world, but you surpass them all!""

—Proverbs 31:10-31 NLT

Rather than list all of the verses, I listed a few. Please grab your Bible to read these in their entirety. This scripture is oftentimes referenced by women who claim to be or seek to be the epitome of the virtuous woman. And also by men who seek out and embrace the woman described in these verses. The dictionary defines virtuous as, "Having or showing high moral standards."[2] Another definition says, "morally excellent."[3] We all have different viewpoints about the virtuous woman and who, and what she is to her family and society. I decided to include my interpretation, taking in both the ancient and modern perspectives and cultural understandings of a woman and wife:

> *The virtuous woman is priceless. She is trusted because she is trustworthy. As a wife, she brings no harm or shame to her spouse, only goodness and peace. When people see her they proclaim her greatness in representing God and her family. She is hardworking, not lazy. She is entrepreneurial. She works hard to provide for herself and her household. She does not waste precious moments with frivolous antics, because she's too busy making "boss moves". In relationships, she focuses her energy on contributing to the partnership. She has a vision of building ladders together to the boldest of dreams. No matter who the breadwinner is in the family, she values, respects, and appreciates the collective earnings.*
>
> *She is not careless with the investment of those earnings. She does not operate with a sense of expectation or entitlement. Her growth brings change, and an ability to adapt and overcome her circumstances. She only gets better with time. She does not let her past dictate her present or her future. She is not petty or retaliatory. She is dependable, walks with dignity, and treats others accordingly. She leans on God in all ways. She takes care of her mind, body, spirit, soul, and finances. She is mindful of her appearance and aims to present herself in a way that glorifies God. She builds people up, never tears them down. She is a giver, not a taker. She speaks from wisdom, through the lessons learned, the lessons shared by the wise, and the guiding words of her Creator. The love, care, and attention that she pours into her family, friends, and the community, brings joy to her family. Through their joy, they rejoice and praise her. In his eyes and through his heart, her husband sees her above all other women in the world. To him, no woman could ever compare to her. She is the crown that an honorable man seeks.*

What do we see here? It is her love and obedience to God, demonstrated through her daily walk, that positions this amazing woman in that great place of honor. When you see her you see God. When you are near her, you feel His energy. This is no easy feat. That is why not every woman can stake claim to this title. The proof is in your walk. Take your first steps, starting this very moment.

Let me shake things up a bit. A conversation in 2018, with Kerric Bennett, led to this deeper thought: This scripture is not only about women, but it's also about men. Scripture says that God is our Husband [read 2 Corinthians 11:2; Isaiah 54:5; Hosea 2:16]. How will you be a virtuous wife to honor our Husband? That is the lens you should use in your human interactions. Think of the things that you desire in a man/woman. Those things should have worth and value; it should be sustainable; it should come from the essence of God.

Consider this—if you want a wife or husband it should never be a goal. Why? Because what happens when you set and later achieve goals? Once the goal is achieved you then focus on a new goal. We sometimes don't work as hard to get the things that we worked to receive. A wife/husband is not to be temporary. That relationship is supposed to resemble your relationship with God, with some unique features that are special to you and your spouse.

The characteristics, beliefs, and values that you desire in a partner are merely your preferences. But Kerric stated that characteristics and the like, should not be seen as a goal. People change as they grow, as they experience the highs and lows of life. If their characteristics, beliefs, and values change, does that mean you discard them and set your mind to finding a new spouse? Imagine if God treated us the same way.

Additionally, you don't want to be in a relationship where you are doing something because you "have to". You should want to. When there is value in a person we do something because we feel that the person is worthy. They are worth it. So doing for them isn't a task, it's just a demonstration of our love. Just like God does for us through His grace. Something to think about. What are your thoughts about all of this?

PRAYER

Father, please mold Your children to be worthy enough to find a partner that You deem virtuous. May we accept the charge to honor, love, respect, cherish, protect, value, and uplift that person. Let us see Your light within them and rather than attempt to cast a shadow or dim the light, help us to find ways to magnify the light so that it may be a blessing to others. Help us to see, realize, and embrace the Truth of You. Please mold us to be honorable, trusting, and trustworthy, confident, and caring. Help us to walk each day as a living testimony to Your greatness and mercy. Let us not rely upon worldly views for what is acceptable or appropriate, but turn us to Your vision Lord.

I humbly pray for You to redirect us from the behaviors, people, places, and things that distract us from greatness. Cleanse us of our transgressions and uplift us to our proper place, so that we may walk according to Your views and ways. I pray to be closer to and in greater alignment with You. In Jesus' name. Amen.

SPEAK YOUR TRUTH

Say the words below and write beside them your truth. You can also use the workbook to write your responses.

I Feel...
I Am...
I Believe...
I Am Grateful For...
I Will Improve...
I Am Proud of Myself Because...
I Will Stay Out of My/God's Way By...
Today I Will Focus More on...
And Focus Less on...
Today I Will ...

GO DEEPER!

When you are ready to go deeper, please refer to **Day 1** in the workbook, **Seek Him: Workbook 1**. It is tied to today's theme and will help you to go farther in your exploration. Each day encourages and challenges you. Each month is more intense. Information on where to purchase the workbook is provided at end of this book. To learn more about the workbook please read the "**Getting The Most From This Book**" section towards the beginning of this book. Are you ready to Go Deeper?

NOTES

Day 2: Be The Tree

The man who trusts in the Lord, whose confidence indeed is The Lord, is blessed. He will be like a tree planted by water: it sends its roots out toward a stream, it doesn't fear when heat comes, and its foliage remains green. It will not worry in a year of drought or cease producing fruit.

—Jeremiah 17:7-8 HCSB

If you are near a tree at this very moment, look at it. If you aren't near a tree, visualize one. Focus and study its structure. Look at its branches and limbs, and how they grow out in various directions. Notice the flowers, seeds, spores, cones, or fruit it bears. Trust me they are there. Can you see its solid strength? Look at the layers of bark that protects the tree from the elements and most animals. Now pan your eyes down and look at the roots and the pattern in which they grow. Do they criss-cross, branch out from each other, or spread like wings? Are they thick, thin, or a combination of both?

The ground and soil are what keep the tree firmly planted. They form the tree's foundation. The water from the Earth and the energy from the sun keep it fed and healthy.

Active Not Passive Prayer

These things are made possible because of God. He is the foundation and source of all living things. We must be productive, committed, and consistent if we want to get the most out of our relationship with Him. We must commit to consistent and productive activity. I say productive because we know how to do busy work while not accomplishing much of anything. That's what it's like when you pray for something and expect God to do everything while you sit back twirling your thumbs.

You pray for a new job but are you applying for them? Are you following up, inquiring about the status of your application or results from your interview? You pray for more income, but you sit in idle only doing the bare minimum. You're not pushing the envelope or preparing yourself. You pray to receive but you rarely give. You pray for a home of your own but you don't take care of and cherish where you're living now. Is it cluttered and/or dirty? Do you pay your rent and utilities on time? You pray for a new car but you don't keep the one that you have immaculate, serviced, and filled with quality gas and oil. You get what you give. Junk for junk and gems for gems.

These examples are all due to a lack of understanding of the connection that you have with God. You may lack appreciation for what God has already given you, and you might have a sense of entitlement. We have all done it. We have all prayed for things but put in little-to-no effort to show God that we were deserving of these things and that we can handle the new and added responsibility. The scriptures tell us to trust God, but we never consider that God too must trust us. Most likely, the reason we don't have something is that God doesn't trust us. He doesn't trust that we can be a great steward of the gifts. We can begin to change that, starting today.

Do you want to see a positive turnaround in your life? Do you want a closer, deeper, stronger connection to God and Jesus Christ? Do you want to be that tree? Then take that step, and keep moving forward with trust in the Lord. Commit to consistent and productive activity each day. Be the tree!

PRAYER

Father, You are my Source and to You, I turn for answers, guidance, and healing. Father, Your all-ness obliterates illness, of all kinds and in all ways, and that is why I focus on You for protection. I'm trying to dig down and root myself to You as my foundation and do so without fear, doubt, and hesitation. I want to be that tree Lord. I want to consistently obey like Jesus, who even when conflicted, obeyed You. Comfort me, Father. Strengthen me so that there is no room for weakness. Help me to de-clutter my mind, body, and my life. I humbly pray for these things in Jesus' name. Amen.

SPEAK YOUR TRUTH

Say the words below and write beside them your truth. You can also use the workbook to write your responses.

I Feel…
I Am…
I Believe…
I Am Grateful For…
I Will Improve…
I Am Proud of Myself Because…
I Will Stay Out of My/God's Way By…
Today I Will Focus More on…
And Focus Less on…
Today I Will …

GO DEEPER!

When you are ready to go deeper, please refer to **Day 2** in the workbook, **Seek Him: Workbook 1**. It is tied to today's theme and will help you to go farther in your exploration. Each day encourages and challenges you. Each month is more intense. Information on where to purchase the workbook is provided at the end of this book. To learn more about the workbook please read the **"Getting The Most From This Book"** section towards the beginning of this book. Are you ready to Go Deeper?

NOTES

Day 3: Release Yourself to God

He was in the world, and the world was created through Him, yet the world did not recognize Him. He came to His own, and His own people did not receive Him.

But to all who did receive Him, He gave them the right to be children of God, to those who believe in His name, who were born, not of blood, or of the will of the flesh, or of the will of man, but of God. The Word became flesh and took up residence among us. We observed His glory, the glory as the One and Only Son from the Father, full of grace and truth.

—John 1:10-14 HCSB

It's hard sometimes to let go of the little bit of control that we think we have. It's difficult pretending that we're releasing ourselves to God. We struggle because more times than we can recall, fear sets in and our surrender is short-lived. The Bible says, shows, and proves that with each step that we take on that walk, the more blessings that we receive. Will you recognize Jesus? Will you follow His lead? Will you trust and believe Him, be obedient, and faithful? Will you release yourself to God?

PRAYER

Father, I open myself to You and my shepherd Jesus Christ. I trust You to restore and comfort me, to heal and enlighten me, and to strengthen and encourage me. I trust You to show me the way and help me be a better person so that I can serve You with 100 percent of me 100 percent of the time. In Jesus' name, I pray. Amen.

SPEAK YOUR TRUTH

Say the words below and write beside them your truth. You can also use the workbook to write your responses.

I Feel...
I Am...
I Believe...
I Am Grateful For...
I Will Improve...
I Am Proud of Myself Because...
I Will Stay Out of My/God's Way By...
Today I Will Focus More on...
And Focus Less on...
Today I Will ...

GO DEEPER!

When you are ready to go deeper, please refer to **Day 3** in the workbook.

NOTES

Day 4: He is All

I am the Lord, and there is no other; there is no God but Me. I will strengthen you, though you do not know Me, so that all may know from the rising of the sun to its setting that there is no one but Me. I am the Lord, and there is no other.

—Isaiah 45:5-6 HCSB

Did God make this crystal clear? You can read it twenty thousand times and it will still be as clear as the first time. He is *IS*. He is *ALL*. He is everything good, great, and special. He is God. None before, none during, and none after. He has you.

PRAYER

Father, these words, written in the book of Isaiah I believe to be true. I don't want to ever consider otherwise. I don't ever again want to question the when, where, why, who, and how when it comes to You. I want to be free and I know that freedom is only possible in and through You. You are all-in-all. My journey will only be successful when I live like You, believing that I am You and You are me. Help me to stop looking elsewhere and start focusing only on You. In Jesus' name, I humbly pray. Amen.

SPEAK YOUR TRUTH

Say the words below and write beside them your truth. You can also use the workbook to write your responses.

I Feel...
I Am...
I Believe...
I Am Grateful For...
I Will Improve...
I Am Proud of Myself Because...
I Will Stay Out of My/God's Way By...
Today I Will Focus More on...
And Focus Less on...
Today I Will ...

GO DEEPER!

When you are ready to go deeper, please refer to **Day 4** in the workbook.

NOTES

Day 5: Your Gifts and Talents

God gave these four young men knowledge and understanding in every kind of literature and wisdom. Daniel also understood visions and dreams of every kind.

—Daniel 1:17 HCSB

God gives us talents and skills, but it is up to us to use them—fully and for good. Don't use your intuition (or insight) to manipulate people or situations. Your gift as a visionary should never oppress or exploit others. Don't take advantage of people with your warm personality and gift of persuasion. Your gift of discernment isn't for causing chaos or conflict. Your gift of gab isn't for starting or spreading gossip. We're supposed to use our gifts for good, to highlight and spread God's Love, and to be the example that Jesus calls us to be.

I have some gifts, talents, and skills that I have placed on the back burner, neglected, and underused. I pray that God frees me from the internal "funk" that has chained me to believe that my behavior is acceptable. To not use my gifts is to tell God that He wasted them, and to tell Jesus that his logic is flawed and unreasonable. I don't know about you, but it doesn't feel good disrespecting God and Jesus. So I'm peeling back these layers of darkness that have served as a facade of contentment. I'm stepping up and stepping out ready to use what God gave me. What are you going to do? Will you stay as-is and come up short? Or will you reposition yourself so that you can make the most of your blessings? God wants you to watch your cup overflow.

PRAYER

Father, You have blessed me with talents, skills, and gifts. Some I flourish in, some I squander, and some I have yet to identify and claim. Father, please help me see, seize, and make the most of these blessings. Help me to push past fear and confusion, and walk boldly in Your Truth. Let me not procrastinate, contemplate, or make excuses. Let me focus on today and not be overwhelmed with tomorrow, or fixated on yesterday. That way I only exert the energy needed to run my daily race. In Your son's name, I pray to You. Amen.

SPEAK YOUR TRUTH

Say the words below and write beside them your truth. You can also use the workbook to write your responses.

- I Feel...
- I Am...
- I Believe...
- I Am Grateful For...
- I Will Improve...
- I Am Proud of Myself Because...
- I Will Stay Out of My/God's Way By...
- Today I Will Focus More on...
- And Focus Less on...
- Today I Will ...

GO DEEPER!

When you are ready to go deeper, please refer to **Day 5** in the workbook.

NOTES

Day 6: Believing and Trusting Jesus

Then the Jews surrounded Him and asked, "How long are You going to keep us in suspense? If You are the Messiah, tell us plainly." "I did tell you and you don't believe," Jesus answered them. "The works that I do in My Father's name testify about Me. But you don't believe because you are not My sheep. My sheep hear My voice, I know them, and they follow Me. I give them eternal life, and they will never perish—ever! No one will snatch them out of My hand. My Father, who has given them to Me, is greater than all. No one is able to snatch them out of the Father's hand. The Father and I are one."

—John 10:24-30 HCSB

Thousands of people doubted Jesus and questioned him repeatedly. No matter how many times he said and demonstrated who he was and to whom he belonged, they doubted him. They were blinded by fear, doubt, frustration, ignorance, arrogance, ego, and jaded beliefs. Even his disciples questioned him many times. He showed them how to heal, yet they still had doubt. Jesus followed God's rules, plans, and ways—not man's. And man, in ignorance, was too blind to see him for who he truly was. Just as man struggles with this today.

Jesus Could Be Walking Amongst Us Right Now

There are millions of people who don't believe in Jesus, and God's works through him. There are many more who flat out don't believe in God. Why expect to see something when you don't believe you will see it? That's the case with blessings and miracles. Being cynical is costly. Jesus could be walking amongst us right now and we wouldn't know. That's because most of us are doubters and conditional believers.

Some people believe that Jesus could only be walking amongst us in grandiose fashion. Visualize a parade of lights and dramatic cloud movements. There would be chariots cascading from the heavens and other extremes. That's not what happened more than 2,000 years ago, so who is to say it won't happen in the same casual fashion it did before? How do you know if the homeless guy you pass each day is not Jesus? He could be sitting back observing our behavior and how we treat his flock? In the **Go Deeper** section following today's prayer, I'm going to stretch your mind and challenge your thinking.

More than 2,000 years ago people doubted Jesus and they could see and touch him. People doubted God because they couldn't see and touch Him. Fast forward to today. How is anything different? This is something humans have struggled with for thousands of years. For hundreds of years, Jews struggled because they could not believe and obey. They were God's chosen, yet they couldn't walk completely in and by faith. They kept backsliding to their old ways.

We're Still Making the Same Foolish Mistakes

Here we are today and guess what? We too are lost sheep in the wilderness. We keep forgetting what He's done for us, what He's doing for us, and what He can still do for us. We don't credit God for all healings. We call blessings "luck" or say that we "did the work". We allow scientists to convince us that certain things couldn't be the works of God. We'll walk right past one of God's less fortunate children without blinking an eye.

Look through the Bible, read your history books, and watch the films and documentaries. See for yourself the twisted history of mankind. We want and we expect, but we don't give 100% of ourselves over to God. Then we have the nerve to wonder why we don't get 100% of what we want when we want it. That is our struggle and why we struggle. Aren't you tired of struggling? To gain your blessings you have to reach your hands outward. You have to move. You have to do something. What are you going to do?

PRAYER
Thank You, Father, for waking me another day. Thank You for the continued blessings. Thank You for the messages You have sent to me through others. I hear them and will follow, and obey. I am ready to take the next step. I am ready to push past fears and put my trust in You that You will take care of everything as You see fit when You see fit. I will not doubt or question You, and if I begin to please stop me short as You know my heart, Lord. I am walking Father with my arms stretched out and my eyes straight ahead. In Jesus' name, I humbly pray. Amen.

SPEAK YOUR TRUTH
Say the words below and write beside them your truth. You can also use the workbook to write your responses.

I Feel...
I Am...
I Believe...
I Am Grateful For...
I Will Improve...
I Am Proud of Myself Because...
I Will Stay Out of My/God's Way By...
Today I Will Focus More on...
And Focus Less on...
Today I Will ...

GO DEEPER!

When you are ready to go deeper, please refer to **Day 6** in the workbook.

NOTES

Day 7: How Are You Investing Your Time?

Whatever you do, do it enthusiastically, as something done for the Lord and not for men, knowing that you will receive the reward of an inheritance from the Lord. You serve the Lord Christ.

—Colossians 3:23-24 HCSB

What if we invested equal time and energy in the tasks that we dreaded as we do the things that we are passionate about? What could we achieve? Where could we go? What could we see? How would our lives change if we passionately jumped into life? It makes you wonder why you keep slow poking around, doesn't it?

You Must Face Your Fears

Those things that we dread and fear aren't going away. They will remain there until we address them until we do our part to put those things to rest. The longer it takes for us to complete the things that we are trying to run from, the greater the mountain it becomes. Even if it's having a difficult but necessary conversation, why delay the inevitable?

Don't let life pass you by. It's okay that we have fears, even Jesus did. But Jesus surrendered to God's will, and as an act of faith, we too must decide to surrender to God. Or surrender to the fear. God's desire is freeing, it's liberating. Anything else is not God.

PRAYER

Father I'm praying for the strength and courage to take the next steps needed to be where You want me to be. I want to step up today and say that from this point on everything that I do will be in Jesus' name. I want to do these things with enthusiasm and passion. I'm not saying that there won't be times when I'm afraid, confused, or reluctant. But I know that with Your will and grace I can confidently push through, conquer, and succeed. I'm tired of being stagnant in areas where You expect my movement and success. I'm tired of being tired. I'm walking forward Father in Jesus' name. Amen.

SPEAK YOUR TRUTH

Say the words below and write beside them your truth. You can also use the workbook to write your responses.

> I Feel...
> I Am...
> I Believe...
> I Am Grateful For...
> I Will Improve...
> I Am Proud of Myself Because...
> I Will Stay Out of My/God's Way By...
> Today I Will Focus More on...
> And Focus Less on...
> Today I Will ...

GO DEEPER!

When you are ready to go deeper, please refer to **Day 7** in the workbook, **Seek Him: Workbook 1**.

NOTES

Day 8: Jesus IS Our Proof

When You did awesome things for which we did not look, You came down, The mountains shook at Your presence. For since the beginning of the world Men have not heard nor perceived by the ear, Nor has the eye seen any God besides You, Who acts for the one who waits for Him. You meet him who rejoices and does righteousness, Who remembers You in Your ways. You are indeed angry, for we have sinned— In these ways we continue; And we need to be saved.

...We all fade as a leaf, And our iniquities, like the wind, Have taken us away. And there is no one who calls on Your name, Who stirs himself up to take hold of You; For You have hidden Your face from us, And have consumed us because of our iniquities. But now, O Lord, You are our Father; We are the clay, and You our potter; And all we are the work of Your hand. Do not be furious, O Lord, Nor remember iniquity forever; Indeed, please look—we all are Your people!

—Isaiah 64:3-9 NKJV

God has done so much for His people for so long, yet what have we done to honor Him? We doubt Him. We pick and choose when we want Him to consciously exist in our lives. We lean towards His messengers for salvation, instead of turning to Him. We would prefer connecting and understanding flesh—that we see—then Spirit that we can't see. Why is that the case, when we know that man is limited in what he can and can't do? Man can only do what God blesses him to do. But we of little faith and limited thinking refuse to accept what Jesus taught about our Father.

Follow The Way of Jesus

Jesus got on the cross, accepted torture and humiliation, and a human death. Then through the resurrection, he proved the power, will, and grace of God our Father. Jesus proved our spiritual connection with God, our metaphysical existence, and that we are more than flesh. But we must evolve, grow, and walk beyond what our small minds can conceive. We must sacrifice what we think we know, and turn to the Truth which can only be taught and delivered by and through God.

God's messengers are here to point us in His direction. It is up to us to make and keep that connection. Jesus is proof of what can be done. It is up to us to develop a level of understanding where we can also demonstrate who and what we are—God's children, the same spiritual DNA—His perfect reflection. When we reach that level of understanding then we will realize that with God there are no limits to what we can do, see, feel, hear, smell, think, or say. Allow Him to mold you into the model you were born to be!

PRAYER

Father, thank You for being a righteous, graceful, forgiving God. Thank You for forgiving us for our limited grasp of what You are, what You do, and what You choose not to do to teach us, spare us, and mold us. You have the will and power to wipe humanity off the face of the earth, but Your spares us. Although we love You conditionally, You love us unconditionally. Thank You, Father. Although we put our trust more in man than we do in You, You still don't love and protect us any less.

You sent Jesus as the ultimate example and reflection of You. Yet your children fail to emulate him. Father, I pray for the vision, strength, courage, and wisdom to walk on Your path. I have never seen You or Jesus. But I choose to follow your lead. I thank You now, Father, for forgiving me for my ignorance, fear, and lack of faith. Please continue to mold me as You see fit. Those moments when I want to complain about my molding process, I will choose instead to trust You. I love You Father. Amen.

SPEAK YOUR TRUTH
Say the words below and write beside them your truth. You can also use the workbook to write your responses.

I Feel...
I Am...
I Believe...
I Am Grateful For...
I Will Improve...
I Am Proud of Myself Because...
I Will Stay Out of My/God's Way By...
Today I Will Focus More on...
And Focus Less on...
Today I Will ...

GO DEEPER!
When you are ready to go deeper, please refer to **Day 8** in the workbook.

NOTES

Day 9: Love is the Perfect Bond of Unity

Above all, put on love — the perfect bond of unity. And let the peace of the Messiah, to which you were also called in one body, control your hearts. Be thankful. Let the message about the Messiah dwell richly among you, teaching and admonishing one another in all wisdom, and singing psalms, hymns, and spiritual songs, with gratitude in your hearts to God. And whatever you do, in word or in deed, do everything in the name of the Lord Jesus, giving thanks to God the Father through Him.

—Colossians 3:14-17 HCSB

Wow, re-read the first verse again. That verse tells us that love and the act of love is the perfect bond of unity. By loving each other we form a bond through good times and bad. Consider if we obeyed the verse as it reads to let Jesus' peace control our hearts. Jesus was the epitome of peace and love. If we let that peace come in and control us how would our lives be and what would be different in our world? Of God's commandments, Jesus said the most important was to love your neighbor as yourself. With his peace and our unified love, would we not see a world that obeyed this command fully?

The next verse tells us to let the message about Jesus and his teachings resonate within us. The message is to be embedded in our minds and hearts so that we can change our ways and help others to change theirs. So that we're all aligned with God's plan and Jesus' way. The verse goes on to tell us to sing with gratitude in our hearts. Even when times get rough, we're supposed to lift our heads and sing as though we're living our best lives. We're to praise God and Jesus for our lives and the opportunity to live them.

Yes, that is difficult when all that you see and feel is consumed by darkness. But even in pitch black shines a light—so sing your praises! Don't wait for others to do it first, you need to leap. The verse concludes with a declaration that we should do and say everything in the name of Jesus, while also thanking God for Jesus. Consider if we did this. How different would our lives be? We would be more selective in the things we did and said. We would consider, "What would Jesus do?" before speaking or acting. Consider that.

PRAYER

Father thank You for this day. No matter what I face today and in the future, I am humbly grateful for my life and each experience. Father, I pray for more patience and a greater sense of discernment. I pray to be quicker to accept and embrace others. I pray that each day I learn to be more like Jesus in speech and my spiritual walk. I want to forgive others quicker. I want to move forward with fewer delays, reach more goals, and see and experience more. I want to bless more people, share more testimonies, and increase my faith beyond question. In Jesus' name, I pray. Amen.

SPEAK YOUR TRUTH

Say the words below and write beside them your truth. You can also use the workbook to write your responses.

I Feel...
I Am...
I Believe...

I Am Grateful For...
I Will Improve...
I Am Proud of Myself Because...
I Will Stay Out of My/God's Way By...
Today I Will Focus More on...
And Focus Less on...
Today I Will ...

GO DEEPER!
When you are ready to go deeper, please refer to **Day 9** in the workbook.

NOTES

Day 10: Protecting Your Heart

Guard your heart above all else, for it determines the course of your life.

—Proverbs 4:23 NLT

When times get rough we show our true self to the world. How do you respond during turmoil? Do you let it drag you down to your lowest depths or do you grab ahold of something and fight your way back to the top? How are you in relationships? Are you putting God first or do you think of your perceived wants and needs first?

If your heart is not aligned with God then you struggle to forgive. Let go of past issues, move forward, and grow. You must guard your heart. Protecting it from internal (self-doubt and fear) and external threats. So that you can respond, rather than always react to life's circumstances. Protecting your heart also insulates you so that you are more receptive and accepting of God's loving guidance.

Don't Be Confused

A protected heart allows you to push back when turmoil surfaces, when fear attempts to creep up and drown you, and when conflict tries to distract you. Don't confuse "protected" with being closed off, disconnected, or cold. It means to not be reckless or thoughtless. It means having the discernment to block the negative energy that would pour into you. You can block the energy by counteracting the negative with positive rebuke. It means leading with God at the forefront of your mind.

Today, won't you take that step towards faith—with the belief that God, as your Protector, has you in His capable Hands? Won't you take the step, knowing that God trusts your ability to be a good steward of His gifts? If He trusts you then why can't you trust Him?

Are you not trustworthy?

PRAYER

Father, thank You for giving me the gift of peace, through any situation that I might face. Thank You for the Word that turns any mess into a miracle; that lifts one up when we're down, and gives us hope when in doubt. I will praise so I can be raised. I Love You Father. I will protect my heart so out of it only comes a reflection of You. I give You all the glory. Amen.

SPEAK YOUR TRUTH

Say the words below and write beside them your truth. You can also use the workbook to write your responses.

> I Feel...
> I Am...
> I Believe...
> I Am Grateful For...
> I Will Improve...
> I Am Proud of Myself Because...
> I Will Stay Out of My/God's Way By...
> Today I Will Focus More on...
> And Focus Less on...
> Today I Will ...

GO DEEPER!

Please refer to **Day 10** in the workbook.

NOTES

Day 11: God's Compassion

As a father has compassion on his children, so the Lord has compassion on those who fear Him.

—Psalms 103:13 HCSB

You know that God's grace has saved you when you have done wrong and He didn't let you fall off of a "cliff". You know that God is protecting you when you avoid or survive a disaster. When you're in pain and this calming energy cloaks you, that's God. God's grace makes all things and experiences in your life possible. You have done nothing to deserve what you have had, what you currently have, and what you may or may not have in the future. Every item that you have, every relationship that you have been in, everything that you consume is only possible because of God's grace. You could never actually buy any of this because even money is only an instrument because God makes it so. All of this is a gift. Now smile and enjoy your day!

PRAYER
Father thank You for this day. Thank You for clearing paths, moving obstacles, and revealing Your Truth. Thank You for Your love, patience, and favor. Thank You for sparing me from punishment. Thank You for showing me each day why my life is so great, and why I am so blessed. No matter how rough my days can get or my life can be, I still smile. It's only because of You. Thank You, Father.

SPEAK YOUR TRUTH

Say the words below and write beside them your truth. You can also use the workbook to write your responses.

I Feel ...
I Am ...
I Believe ...
I Am Grateful For ...
I Will Improve ...
I Am Proud of Myself Because ...
I Will Stay Out of My/God's Way By ...
Today I Will Focus More on...
And Focus Less on...
Today I Will ...

GO DEEPER!

Please refer to **Day 11** in the workbook.

NOTES

Day 12: Anticipation

For we are God's workmanship created in Christ Jesus to do good works, which God prepared in advance for us to do.

—Ephesians 2:10 NIV

Expect good things to come your way. Expect God to handle all your needs, knowing that your issues were not a surprise to Him as they were for You. God has huge plans for each of us. It's what we do each day that determines whether we seize the opportunities or let them squander. Expect greatness and boldness, because God is great and bold. Are you ready to fully embrace God's abundance of blessings?

PRAYER

Father, thank You for setting me free. I release my faith to You knowing that old things have passed away and You will make old things new things. Release me of past hurt, for today I am to be present with You and free from yesterday. I receive a new beginning today and a fresh new vision for my life. Thank You for directing and ordering my steps as only You can. I bless and praise You today and always. Amen.

SPEAK YOUR TRUTH

Say the words below and write beside them your truth. You can also use the workbook to write your responses.

I Feel...
I Am...
I Believe...
I Am Grateful For...
I Will Improve...
I Am Proud of Myself Because...
I Will Stay Out of My/God's Way By...
Today I Will Focus More on...
And Focus Less on...
Today I Will ...

GO DEEPER!
Please refer to **Day 12** in the workbook.

NOTES

Day 13: Standing Tall in Your Conviction

"There are some Jews you have appointed to manage the province of Babylon: Shadrach, Meshach, and Abednego. These men have ignored you, the king; they do not serve your gods or worship the gold statue you have set up." Then in a furious rage Nebuchadnezzar gave orders to bring in Shadrach, Meshach, and Abednego. So these men were brought before the king. Nebuchadnezzar asked them, "Shadrach, Meshach, and Abednego, is it true that you don't serve my gods or worship the gold statue I have set up? Now if you're ready, when you hear the sound of the horn, flute, zither, lyre, harp, drum, and every kind of music, fall down and worship the statue I made. But if you don't worship it, you will immediately be thrown into a furnace of blazing fire — and who is the god who can rescue you from my power?" Shadrach, Meshach, and Abednego replied to the king, "Nebuchadnezzar, we don't need to give you an answer to this question. If the God we serve exists, then He can rescue us from the furnace of blazing fire, and He can rescue us from the power of you, the king. But even if He does not rescue us, we want you as king to know that we will not serve your gods or worship the gold statue you set up."

—Daniel 3:12-18 HCSB

Would you stand tall in your convictions like Shadrach, Meshach, and Abednego? Would you have the courage to look directly in the eyes of a person who could take your life, and tell them what Nebuchadnezzar heard that day? Do you stand bold as a soldier for Christ? If a gun was pointed at your head and you were told that you either worship another god or be killed, what would you do? What would you do if your choices were to serve another human as you would serve God, or be tortured or killed? Be honest, what would you say and do?

If someone placed a pile of money, gold and diamonds stacked high on a huge conference table and gave you the option of taking it all and turning your back on God, or walking away and watching them wipe out your bank accounts and other assets, leaving you penniless, what would be your decision? Be honest, did you contemplate even for a few minutes or seconds? Did you consider pretending to be a loyal worshipper of another god (to spare your life and limbs) but still secretly worship God? Did you consider serving a human master instead of God? Could you justify it to spare your life?

Could you convince yourself that you are only pretending to rebuke God? What about when it came to the money? Did you ever at any point think that you could tell God your plans to pretend to rebuke Him while taking the money? It's been done many times over thousands of years. I'm not saying it's right or wrong. I'm reflecting and posing questions for you to consider. What is our breaking point? Negotiation point? Fake it point? Can we publicly denounce Him then risk privately worshipping Him? Shadrach, Meshach, and Abednego didn't even consider faking it for the king and others, they said *"No. Do what you're going to do, but we're staying true to our God!"* That's deep. That's bold. That's what we call conviction.

PRAYER

Father, I pray for faith, strength, courage, and conviction to never back down from serving and worshipping You. I pray that even if faced with death or torture that I would never turn my back on You. Father even if tempted by the riches of the world, I pray for the fullness within to resist. I know that You are always with me and that even if I don't see any action from You, there is a reason that I'm not to question. I want to not question You, only trust You. In Jesus' name, I pray for more strength and courage to be a better soldier in Your army. Amen.

SPEAK YOUR TRUTH

Say the words below and write beside them your truth. You can also use the workbook to write your responses.

> I Feel…
> I Am…
> I Believe…
> I Am Grateful For…
> I Will Improve…
> I Am Proud of Myself Because…
> I Will Stay Out of My/God's Way By…
> Today I Will Focus More on…
> And Focus Less on…
> Today I Will …

GO DEEPER!

Please refer to **Day 13** in the workbook.

NOTES

Day 14: Running God's Race, Not Man's

Let us run with endurance the race that is set before us looking unto Jesus, the author and finisher of our faith.

—Hebrews 12:1-2 NKJV

We must remember to keep God first in our lives. No decisions should be made until after we've prayed, sought guidance, and reflected. Instead, we're quick to not be beaten in competition for proving our "rightness" in a situation. The only thing right is God's Word. If we don't incorporate it into our lives we'll always be wrong!

PRAYER

Father, I humbly come to You giving You all that I am. I choose to keep my eyes on You and allow You to work in my heart and mind. I declare that I am free from the competition today. I relinquish my desire to find and make a path of my own. I know that all I need to do is follow Yours. I thank You for your continued patience and love. As Your clay, I know that as You mold me I can sometimes be a headache. I love you Lord for loving me. Amen.

SPEAK YOUR TRUTH

Say the words below and write beside them your truth. You can also use the workbook to write your responses.

I Feel...
I Am...
I Believe...
I Am Grateful For...
I Will Improve...
I Am Proud of Myself Because...
I Will Stay Out of My/God's Way By...
Today I Will Focus More on...
And Focus Less on...
Today I Will ...

GO DEEPER!

Please refer to **Day 14** in the workbook.

NOTES

Day 15: Pray For The Stubborn

The chief priests and the whole Sanhedrin were looking for false testimony against Jesus so they could put Him to death. But they could not find any, even though many false witnesses came forward...

—Matthew 26:59-60 HCSB

We all will face an attack on some level. We may know someone who wants to snatch the "rug" from beneath our feet or push us into a pit of despair. It is our relationship with God that determines the outcome. Is our relationship with God fear-based or love-based? Are we more focused on self, or on God and our desire to glorify Him?

Continue reading the remaining passages of Matthew and see Jesus' reaction and responses to those who verbally, psychologically, and physically attacked him. He knew who he was and to whom he belonged. He knew that no matter what those people did to his body, they would never have and control his mind. They could never remove him from his rightful place with God. They could never change his mind about his Father. It never mattered what people said to him or about him. Nor did it matter what people did to him. What mattered to Jesus was what God said and did. That is the place we all need to be. Turning things over to God, with our focus only on serving Him and staying true to Him. Staying true to God is the only way we can remain true to ourselves. His Truth is the only Truth.

With growth comes change. It's inevitable. You can't grow without changing. You can change without growing. Yes indeed. Backslide and see how you change, possibly for the worse. Without strengthening yourself through God, you will change in all the wrong ways. But change through growth is always an awesome thing. It's always a God-thing. You can't get better without God's will and grace. You have to open yourself up to recognize and marvel in this great blessing. As Jesus prayed for his critics—pray for those culprits who don't want to change their ways. Pray that they see and feel God's light and allow Him to move them to a higher level of thinking. Then pray the same for yourself. Stop dwelling in the past. Stop making excuses for not getting your life together. Stop letting past hurts keep you from growing, changing, and living God's plan—on purpose!

PRAYER
Father calm the waters, settle the restlessness, heal the hurt, and mend the broken. I pray for myself and your children. May we walk peacefully—free from the confusion and chaos of the enemy. Let us have the strength to withstand all attacks. Let us seek out change and growth through You. Remove the fear that would hold us back. Remove the fear that would have us sabotage our lives. In Jesus' name, I humbly pray. Amen.

SPEAK YOUR TRUTH
Say the words below and write beside them your truth. You can also use the workbook to write your responses.

I Feel...
I Am...
I Believe...
I Am Grateful For...
I Will Improve...

I Am Proud of Myself Because...
I Will Stay Out of My/God's Way By...
Today I Will Focus More on...
And Focus Less on...
Today I Will ...

GO DEEPER!
Please refer to **Day 15** in the workbook.

NOTES

Day 16: Believing in God

When you pray and ask for something, believe that you have received it, and you will be given what you ask for.

—Mark 11:24 GNT

True faith comes with believing before you see it. It comes from thanking God for your blessings long before you receive them. You believe in Him, what He can and has done, and what you believe He will still do for you. God will bless me with a husband who is loving, faithful, nurturing, supportive and devoted.

I have faith that this man is a good steward, provider, protector, and honorable servant of the Lord. I have faith that God will bless me with children. I have faith that He will bless me with the financial means to take care of my family. I believe that God will always provide me with the means to reach and help the masses. By helping them, I can share God's greatness and in turn help build His Kingdom. I believe that God will put before me the solutions to all of my financial issues, and handle my debt. He is waiting for me to prove that I can be a good and responsible steward.

I truly believe that He will free me from certain situations that would be unbearable if He weren't in my life. If He weren't my rock and salvation, my shade tree and fountain of life, I don't know what I would do. I believe in Him because of who He is and because of His incredible track record. He may not have always given me everything that I asked for but I'm grateful for what He has given me. I am grateful for my relationship with Him. I know that every thought and every word that I speak He is always listening.

PRAYER

Father, thank You for my wondrous gifts. Thank You for the life that You have given me to see, learn, experience, and express Your love and greatness. I am reassured by my faith in You. I can thank You now for the things that I desire because You will always provide what I need and when I need it. Thank You for my excellent spiritual, mental, and physical health. I thank You for the excellent health of my loved ones. Thank You for placing me in situations where I can help Your children. Some who have lost their way, some whose faith is slipping, and some who still hope to know You.

Thank You for providing me with the financial means to provide for my family. Thank You for the home that provides shelter and security. Thank You for my physical and spiritual food. Thank You, Father, for blessing me with children and taking care of their needs. Thank You for opening doors and windows of opportunity. Thank You, Father, for loving me even those days when I am not loving. I look to Your son, Jesus, as the example and I strive to walk as He did and has. I humbly bow and pray to You in Jesus' name. Amen.

SPEAK YOUR TRUTH

Say the words below and write beside them your truth. You can also use the workbook to write your responses.

> I Feel…
> I Am…
> I Believe…
> I Am Grateful For…
> I Will Improve…
> I Am Proud of Myself Because…
> I Will Stay Out of My/God's Way By…
> Today I Will Focus More on…

And Focus Less on...
Today I Will ...

GO DEEPER!
Please refer to **Day 16** in the workbook.

NOTES

Day 17: God Rescues

Then King Nebuchadnezzar jumped up in alarm. He said to his advisers, "Didn't we throw three men, bound, into the fire?" "Yes, of course, Your Majesty," they replied to the king. He exclaimed, "Look! I see four men, not tied, walking around in the fire unharmed; and the fourth looks like a son of the gods."

When the satraps, prefects, governors, and the king's advisers gathered around, they saw that the fire had no effect on the bodies of these men: not a hair of their heads was singed, their robes were unaffected, and there was no smell of fire on them. Nebuchadnezzar exclaimed, "Praise to the God of Shadrach, Meshach, and Abednego! He sent His angel and rescued His servants who trusted in Him. They violated the king's command and risked their lives rather than serve or worship any god except their own God.

—Daniel 3:24, 27-28 HCSB

No matter what someone else perceives to be true, God determines how things play out. You have a choice—to follow Jesus on God's path—or believe and follow the enemy. Don't allow doubters to fill your mind with their nonsense. Don't let cheaters steal your joy. Don't let anyone enslave your mind. Be free in God.

PRAYER

Father, no matter what I face in life You will deal with it. My enemies have no power or control over me. This walk is between us Lord. You determine the details and I focus on obeying. I will keep praying and pushing myself each day. I will keep studying, believing in Jesus' teachings, and being the person that You expect. Giving You all the glory. Amen.

SPEAK YOUR TRUTH

Say the words below and write beside them your truth. You can also use the workbook to write your responses.

> I Feel…
> I Am…
> I Believe…
> I Am Grateful For…
> I Will Improve…
> I Am Proud of Myself Because…
> I Will Stay Out of My/God's Way By…
> Today I Will Focus More on…
> And Focus Less on…
> Today I Will …

GO DEEPER!

Please refer to **Day 17** in the workbook.

NOTES

Day 18: Wisdom

Give instruction to a wise man, and he will be yet wiser: teach a just man, and he will increase in learning. The fear of the Lord is the beginning of wisdom: and the knowledge of the holy is understanding. For by me thy days shall be multiplied, and the years of thy life shall be increased. If thou be wise, thou shalt be wise for thyself: but if thou scornest, thou alone shalt bear it.

—Proverbs 9:9-12 KJV

Never be so into yourself that you fail to realize that every second of your life is a learning experience. It doesn't matter how many years you have worked in a career, or how many books you have read or written. It doesn't matter how many certificates, degrees, or awards that you have earned. When your confidence turns to arrogance, you tell God that you believe your wisdom is not by His will and grace. Humble yourself and be a sponge to His wisdom. Open yourself to instruction led by His messengers. Don't limit your blessings by thinking and acting as though "It's all about me!" Make sure that you pay forward your learned lessons. You might rid them of learning things the hard way.

PRAYER
Father, thank You for keeping Your promises and supplying my needs. Thank You for opening my eyes so that I might see with clarity. Thank You for helping

me to hear Your voice, and discern what others are saying and doing. Thank You for humbling me so that I might be open to instruction, and through You be wiser and faithful. Thank You for blessing me with life and the years that I have been on this earth. Thank You for many more to come. Amen.

SPEAK YOUR TRUTH

Say the words below and write beside them your truth. You can also use the workbook to write your responses.

I Feel...
I Am...
I Believe...
I Am Grateful For...
I Will Improve...
I Am Proud of Myself Because...
I Will Stay Out of My/God's Way By...
Today I Will Focus More on...
And Focus Less on...
Today I Will ...

GO DEEPER!

Please refer to **Day 18** in the workbook.

NOTES

Day 19: Patience

The glory of this present house will be greater than the glory of the former house, says the LORD almighty and in this place I will grant you peace.

—Haggai 2:9 NIV

Wait on the Lord, and He will come through. Get on His time and stop obsessing about man's time. What is meant for you will be, but only at the time that God determines. God is not measured by or limited to the concept of time. He has already mapped out the steps.

There are key factors that will and must take place before they manifest in your life. What you had in the past won't compare to what He is providing and molding You for today and tomorrow. Open your arms and receive your blessings. Know that you deserve them because God is giving them to you. He will never give you what He has in store for someone else, and vice versa. Rejoice and testify in His name!

PRAYER
Father, thank You for being a God of increase. I prepare my heart and mind to receive the increase and blessings You have in store for me. I surrender every area of my mind, will, and emotion as I wait on You. What I had in my past will be overshadowed by what You are delivering to me in the present day. I thank You now in advance. Amen.

SPEAK YOUR TRUTH

Say the words below and write beside them your truth. You can also use the workbook to write your responses.

I Feel...
I Am...
I Believe...
I Am Grateful For...
I Will Improve...
I Am Proud of Myself Because...
I Will Stay Out of My/God's Way By...
Today I Will Focus More on...
And Focus Less on...
Today I Will ...

GO DEEPER!

Please refer to **Day 19** in the workbook.

NOTES

Day 20: God's Command

An officer gives a command. But his soldiers stumble, as they hasten to build a shelter to protect themselves against rocks thrown down from the city wall.

—Nahum 2:5 CEV

God determines the right way and the right time. When we go against Him we end up like the officer and his soldiers—completely exposed to attack from the enemy. We must be "suited and booted" (as the saying goes) with God's armor draped and mounted over us. We must constantly carry our shields, protecting ourselves from attack. We must listen to that small voice in our head that whispers the way—then we must follow as obedient soldiers.

If you want to know the difference between the "liar's"[4] voice and God's, it's simple. The liar would never encourage you to do something that would strengthen you, and make you a better person. The liar would never encourage you to help build God's Kingdom. Temptation is never God. Vanity, pride, ego, and infidelity are not the principles and qualities of God. So a whispered message seasoned with any of these attributes can only be coming from one place—the "liar". Don't let someone or something else distract you from God's plans for your life. Lest you find yourself metaphorically stoned and without shelter!

PRAYER

Father, thank You for protecting me from myself and the attacks of others. I pray that my mind and heart are always focused on You, obeying You, and following the path that You have intended for me. Disobedience leads to chaos, even in the lives of the fittest and trained. I choose to do right by You and follow Your commands. Protect my mind and heart from both known and unknown enemies. I thank You for Your grace, Father. Amen.

SPEAK YOUR TRUTH

Say the words below and write beside them your truth. You can also use the workbook to write your responses.

I Feel…
I Am…
I Believe…
I Am Grateful For…
I Will Improve…
I Am Proud of Myself Because…
I Will Stay Out of My/God's Way By…
Today I Will Focus More on…
And Focus Less on…
Today I Will …

GO DEEPER!

Please refer to **Day 20** in the workbook.

NOTES

Day 21: Glorify God

My lips will glorify You because Your faithful love is better than life. So I will praise You as long as I live; at Your name, I will lift up my hands.

—Psalms 63:3-4 HCSB

Thank God, for your life and for being blessed with another day here on Earth. No matter what you are going through, know that God loves you, and hasn't left you. You are never alone, even when you look in a room and only see yourself. If you are lonely then all you need to do is pick up your Bible, or turn on some soul-stirring music, or sit quietly and pray.

It's amazing how His presence is felt in those precious moments. If you have never tried it, then start right now. After you finish reading this message do one of the three things that I mentioned above. Then post a comment on my blog or social media feeds about your experience. The deeper your connection with God the more you will find comfort during your (perceived) time of aloneness. That is because you are more perceptive to Him, and take the time to see and appreciate all that you have to be grateful for in life. It's an amazing and rewarding experience. With all that He is and all that He does, every single day you should glorify Him!

PRAYER

There is nothing better than loving You and being loved by You Lord. The love I receive from others is channeled from You. The love I give to others comes from You. I'm grateful and honored to follow Jesus to be better connected to You. Of all the names that You are called, Father and Father-Mother suit You best. My nurturer and protector, my Heavenly Parent, I lovingly thank You. Amen.

SPEAK YOUR TRUTH

Say the words below and write beside them your truth. You can also use the workbook to write your responses.

I Feel...
I Am...
I Believe...
I Am Grateful For...
I Will Improve...
I Am Proud of Myself Because...
I Will Stay Out of My/God's Way By...
Today I Will Focus More on...
And Focus Less on...
Today I Will ...

GO DEEPER!

Please refer to **Day 21** in the workbook.

NOTES

Day 22: Learning From Our Elders

But as for you, speak the things which are proper for sound doctrine: that the older men be sober, reverent, temperate, sound in faith, in love, in patience; the older women likewise, that they be reverent in behavior, not slanderers, not given to much wine, teachers of good things— that they admonish the young women to love their husbands, to love their children, to be discreet, chaste, homemakers, good, obedient to their own husbands, that the word of God may not be blasphemed.

Likewise, exhort the young men to be sober-minded, in all things showing yourself to be a pattern of good works; in doctrine showing integrity, reverence, incorruptibility, sound speech that cannot be condemned, that one who is an opponent may be ashamed, having nothing evil to say of you.

—Titus 2:1-8 NKJV

Notice anything amazing about this Bible passage? What about the fact that older and younger people don't interact as we did in the past? How often do you sit down with an elderly person and apply the wisdom that they shared in your daily life? What's stopping you besides yourself? Pick up a phone or make a drive, and sit down and soak up the wisdom that God has blessed them with. Trust me, you will receive blessings!

PRAYER

Father, show us how to reconnect our older men and women with our younger men and women. Let those youthful in age turn to their older and wiser elders for counsel, direction, and support. Let these elders be planted firmly in Your Word and light so that they guide as You would expect. Let Your younger children be receptive to this guidance. Let them see it as an opportunity to learn how to become more loving, patient, kind, responsible, and understanding. Warm our hearts Lord so that this may be a reality for many and not only a few. Let us see Your intent. Let us receive Your blessings. Amen.

SPEAK YOUR TRUTH

Say the words below and write beside them your truth. You can also use the workbook to write your responses.

> I Feel...
> I Am...
> I Believe...
> I Am Grateful For...
> I Will Improve...
> I Am Proud of Myself Because...
> I Will Stay Out of My/God's Way By...
> Today I Will Focus More on...
> And Focus Less on...
> Today I Will ...

GO DEEPER!

Please refer to **Day 22** in the workbook.

NOTES

Day 23: Waiting for God

For the vision is yet for an appointed time.

—Habakkuk 2:3 KJV

Vision is the big picture outlook of where and what you want to be in the future. God places these images in our minds so that we can see the potential of what lies ahead if we choose to pursue the path. Many of us rush to reach the vision before it has fully formed in our minds. We attempt to cut corners and take shortcuts. We don't realize that we're not prepared to reach that finish line. We haven't yet conditioned our mind, body, and spirit to endure the rigorous tests that life will bring.

God knows when the time will come. He knows when you are ready. He will provide you with the resources to build the physical and spiritual muscles that you need to persevere and succeed. We must surrender to His ways, His plans, His timing, and His truth. To surrender you must let go of the things, people, ideas, and feelings that are holding you back. You have to let go of everything that will hold you back. God says that we can have our hearts desire. The question is whether we want to let go so that we're freed to grab ahold of what He has for us. We have choices. Let go, patiently wait for Him, be obedient to His direction, and then let Him do what only He can.

PRAYER

Father, thank You for loving me. Thank You for choosing me. Thank You for placing me in the right place for my provisions to show up, at the right time. Thank You for giving me grace and peace of mind. Remove my fears so that it won't steal the destiny You have planned. Amen.

SPEAK YOUR TRUTH

Say the words below and write beside them your truth. You can also use the workbook to write your responses.

> I Feel...
> I Am...
> I Believe...
> I Am Grateful For...
> I Will Improve...
> I Am Proud of Myself Because...
> I Will Stay Out of My/God's Way By...
> Today I Will Focus More on...
> And Focus Less on...
> Today I Will ...

GO DEEPER!

Please refer to **Day 23** in the workbook.

NOTES

Day 24: The Answers Are Inside of You

The king declared to Daniel, whose name was Belteshazzar, Are you able to make known to me the dream that I have seen and its interpretation? Daniel answered the king and said, No wise men, enchanters, magicians, or astrologers can show to the king the mystery that the king has asked, but there is a God in heaven who reveals mysteries, and he has made known to King Nebuchadnezzar what will be in the latter days....

—Daniel 2:26-28 ESV

Daniel told the king that the answers to his dreams could only be revealed by God, not him or anyone or anything else. Stop looking to man-made concepts, magic, and tomfoolery to answer your questions about the unknown. The answers are inside of you. Ask God and He will reveal them to you. Yes, it really is that simple. You first must believe that you have your own unique relationship with God and Jesus. Until you reach that point of understanding, you will always refer to everything and everyone else.

PRAYER

Father thank You for being my Source for all that I ever need. I know that I can talk to You whenever and wherever I am. Whether that be in the car, elevator, at home, in my office, walking down the street, sitting in the park. I can do in silence or aloud, no matter how I do it You are always there for me. Thank You. I don't need astrologers, a talisman, or any other source to answer the mysteries of life. Especially my life. All I need is You. When I'm puzzled by my dreams I can turn to You for answers. Thank You, Father. Amen.

SPEAK YOUR TRUTH

Say the words below and write beside them your truth. You can also use the workbook to write your responses.

> I Feel...
> I Am...
> I Believe...
> I Am Grateful For...
> I Will Improve...
> I Am Proud of Myself Because...
> I Will Stay Out of My/God's Way By...
> Today I Will Focus More on...
> And Focus Less on...
> Today I Will ...

GO DEEPER!

Please refer to **Day 24** in the workbook.

NOTES

Day 25: God's Faithfulness

Ask, and it will be given to you; seek, and you will find; knock, and it will be opened to you. For everyone who asks receives, and he who seeks finds, and to him who knocks it will be opened.
—Matthew 7:7-8 NIV

What we need most in life can only come from one source—our heavenly Father. Reach out to Him and He will provide. The first huge step requires that we believe He will do it each and every time as promised. What will it take for you to have total faith in Him?

PRAYER
Father, thank You for always providing for me. Thank You for Your faithfulness. Open my eyes and show me what You see. Help me to take the vice grip off my thinking, so that I can receive everything that You have in store for my future. Free me from my fear. So that I will have faith that whenever I ask, seek, and knock—You will always give, reveal, and open doors so that I may have full access to the blessings You have in store for me. Amen.

SPEAK YOUR TRUTH
Say the words below and write beside them your truth. You can also use the workbook to write your responses.

I Feel...

I Am...
I Believe...
I Am Grateful For...
I Will Improve...
I Am Proud of Myself Because...
I Will Stay Out of My/God's Way By...
Today I Will Focus More on...
And Focus Less on...
Today I Will ...

GO DEEPER!
Please refer to **Day 25** in the workbook.

NOTES

Day 26: Let the Storm Pass

And there arose a great storm of wind, and the waves beat into the ship, so that it was now full. And he was in the hinder part of the ship, asleep on a pillow: and they awake him, and say unto him, Master, carest thou not that we perish? And he arose, and rebuked the wind, and said unto the sea, Peace, be still. And the wind ceased, and there was a great calm. And he said unto them, Why are ye so fearful? how is it that ye have no faith? And they feared exceedingly, and said one to another, What manner of man is this, that even the wind and the sea obey him?

—Mark 4:37-41 KJV

Sit in silence and let the storm pass, rather than worry how it will affect you. If you truly believe that God is your all-in-all, your protector, and your guide then have faith in Him and His Son. Trust God and Jesus to lead the way. If you're going to walk in fear, not faith, then why pray? If you're going to worry instead of standing firm in your convictions, then why continue to pray? If you're consistently in prayer, then why be fearful or worried? You can't straddle the fence. You can't live in both realms. Either you are faithful or fearful. Choose.

PRAYER

Father, quiet me when I begin to utter fear-based words, and when thoughts of fear begin to surface in my mind. Show me how to stop, relax, release, and not be concerned with troubled waters. For they don't last long and are never a sign that You aren't with me. I want to be more like Jesus. I want to rest during the storms that take place in my life. I want the peace and surety that all is well, even when the mind and eyes see otherwise. I thank You now for these blessings Father. In Jesus' name. Amen.

SPEAK YOUR TRUTH

Say the words below and write beside them your truth. You can also use the workbook to write your responses.

> I Feel…
> I Am…
> I Believe…
> I Am Grateful For…
> I Will Improve…
> I Am Proud of Myself Because…
> I Will Stay Out of My/God's Way By…
> Today I Will Focus More on…
> And Focus Less on…
> Today I Will …

GO DEEPER!

Please refer to **Day 26** in the workbook.

NOTES

Day 27: Pain

In thee, O Lord, do I put my trust; let me never be ashamed: deliver me in thy righteousness...For thou art my rock and my fortress; therefore for thy name's sake lead me, and guide me...Have mercy upon me, O Lord, for I am in trouble: mine eye is consumed with grief, yea, my soul and my belly...Make thy face to shine upon thy servant: save me for thy mercies' sake.

—Psalm 31:1,3,9,16 KJV

God is always connected to us. When your belly aches with pain there is something you're not seeing. Look and listen closely to God's guidance. Ask Him to reveal His truths so you can be set free.

PRAYER
Father, inside I feel pain. Open my eyes. What am I not seeing? Please release me. Please remove those things and people from my life, both known and unknown, that do me harm. Show them the path away from me so that my focus is on You and building Your Kingdom. Amen.

SPEAK YOUR TRUTH
Say the words below and write beside them your truth. You can also use the workbook to write your responses.

I Feel...
I Am...
I Believe...
I Am Grateful For...
I Will Improve...
I Am Proud of Myself Because...
I Will Stay Out of My/God's Way By...
Today I Will Focus More on...
And Focus Less on...
Today I Will ...

GO DEEPER!
Please refer to **Day 27** in the workbook.

NOTES

Day 28: What the Lord Requires of You

Mankind, He has told you what is good and what it is the Lord requires of you: to act justly, to love faithfulness, and to walk humbly with your God.

—Micah 6:8 HCSB

ACTING JUSTLY

Acting justly can be difficult when bias comes in. And when things become so personal that you are blinded. It means looking at a situation and then moving forward with no bias. There must be actual or perceived fairness in decisions made. If not, how can it possibly be just and pure? Seeking revenge can never truly be just. Especially since God said that vengeance would always be His. The only way to even the scales is by stepping back and watching God do His thing.

LOVING FAITHFULNESS

Loving faithfulness is not as easy as it sounds. As humans, we have had a bad track record of being unfaithful. Of course, there is a lack of commitment to God, we are in general very wishy-washy in our ability to stay true to Him. It is no surprise that we're unfaithful to other humans. We don't seem to have an authentic love for faithfulness. It is not just our faithfulness to love God, but our faithfulness to love each other.

We should strive to be faithful, loyal, and committed to our relationships. We should never excuse ourselves to stray and cheat on our spouse/significant other. We must love this faithfulness. We must love being and seeing a commitment so strong that it can only be broken by God. It is not acceptable to say, *"That's what men do"* or *"What do you expect? He's just a man"* or even, *"Boys will be boys"*.

There are relationship levels that we progress through. We start with casually dating. It progresses to a stage of courting. Then it intensifies into greater levels of commitment that can lead to marriage. As we grow up the relationship ladder, the more committed and faithful we are to become. There are no sound excuses and no reasons to stray. If you don't think you can be faithful then you need to leave the relationship. Don't be selfish and hold on to someone. Could it be that because of our lack of faithfulness that we fail both in our relationship to God and His children? This can also be why many of us fail our families and children, fail in our careers and in reaching our goals. We aren't faithful. We can change this lackluster reputation of ours.

WALK HUMBLY

The third requirement that many of us fall on our faces attempting to do—walk humbly. Our definition of humbleness changes by the situation. To be humble we are never bragging, boasting, mocking, or looking down on others. A good test of this is when you interact with a person who works in hospitality, like at a restaurant or hotel. How do you treat the server, busser, valet, housekeeping staff? How do you view them in comparison to yourself? I strive to always treat people who work in service jobs better than I would like them to treat me. I am a servant of God, so in my role, I am serving all who I encounter.

It doesn't matter what the so-called pecking order is in life, no one is above or beneath me in my eyes—we are all God's children. I will not talk down to, mistreat, or humiliate a person. I will not misuse the power God has given me to do good to live well. My former and current employees would attest to this. Vendors and contractors who work with me now would also say that this is true. I am humbled to be served and to be of service. Walking humbly means that we should be grateful for every penny that God blesses us with, for every win that we receive, for every deal that we close, and for all of the things that we have. It is only because of God that we have what we have. Be humbled. Walk humbly. Act justly. Love faithfulness.

PRAYER
Father, You know my heart and my intentions. I pray that I always act justly, love faithfulness, and walk humbly with You. Correct my steps if ever I stray. I pray that those I love do what is required so as not to disappoint You. Lift us up to do right, live right, and reflect You fully. In Jesus' name, I pray to You. Amen.

SPEAK YOUR TRUTH
Say the words below and write beside them your truth. You can also use the workbook to write your responses.

- I Feel...
- I Am...
- I Believe...
- I Am Grateful For...
- I Will Improve...
- I Am Proud of Myself Because...
- I Will Stay Out of My/God's Way By...
- Today I Will Focus More on...
- And Focus Less on...
- Today I Will ...

GO DEEPER!
Please refer to **Day 28** in the workbook.

NOTES

Day 29: God's Protection

Then I said, "Ah, Lord GOD! Behold, I do not know how to speak, For I am [only] a young man." But the LORD said to me, "Do not say, 'I am [only] a young man,' Because everywhere I send you, you shall go, And whatever I command you, you shall speak. Do not be afraid of them [or their hostile faces], For I am with you [always] to protect you and deliver you," says the LORD.

—Jeremiah 1:4-8 AMP

Past, present, and future, God has it covered. He knows what we have done, what we are doing, and what we will do. He desires that we do good things. He wants us to speak good towards others and about our situations. He wants us to think good thoughts about ourselves and our loved ones, but also about people we have issues with. This also means thinking good thoughts about people we don't know pass judgment on. God always gives us choices. He leads us to where we need to be, but it is up to us to make the right decision. It is up to us to trust and believe in Him; to have faith in Him to provide us with the right thoughts and words to live by. If you have to second guess something you are thinking, saying or doing, then most likely it is not of God. Stop and pray for enlightenment. Then do as you're told. If you say or do something that you can quickly see is negative, immediately apologize.

Find a way to undo your wrong to make things right. Don't hesitate. Don't say, "*Well what's done is done, there's nothing I can do now*," because that simply isn't true. What if God did us that way? What if He was so nonchalant about things? What if He didn't send His angels to help you? What if He didn't whisper in your ear, "*Don't walk in there*," but instead just let things happen? What if after something happened He didn't provide the means to make things right?

I can't recall every single time that God has saved me from situations that would have caused me great physical and emotional harm. But those moments I can recall I am deeply honored, and I humbly send my thanks to Him. Before the age of three, I was almost in a major accident that could have resulted in paralysis or death. I ignored my dad when he told me to stop playing on some bleachers. I slipped through one of the openings and was aiming headfirst for one of the metal beams. But with God's guiding hand, my dad saved me in the nick of time. A second time (around the same age) I was electrocuted and could have died, but I didn't. I was scared, smoky, hands were black and trembling, and my hair was a big puffball on my head, but other than that I was okay. God's will and grace.

Around age five I cut my hand severely with a steak knife, trying to cut an orange. I bled so profusely that I left a trail of blood from the kitchen to the upstairs bathroom. All three times God told me to stop doing what I was doing. All three times He had my father come speak to me and tell me to stop, and all three times I did things my way. Even during the hand-cutting incident, He sent my mother to tell me "*no*", but I ignored those words of caution. In my immature mind, I was a big kid and I could do it!

After my experiences over 40 years ago, I can say that I learned my lesson. I never played on bleachers again. I practice safety first with sharp objects, and I have great respect for electricity. I don't play around with electrical outlets. What if God had been nonchalant about the things I was doing between ages three through five? Can you imagine? I have to believe that He has great things planned for me here. I believe that He wasn't going to allow my curiosity and ignorance to keep me from fulfilling my mission. I thank Him. Take this moment to thank Him for getting you this far. Thank Him for the journey that you have waiting ahead of you.

PRAYER
Father, long before I was conceived in my human mother's womb You knew me. You have always known what kind of person that I would be, how I would live my life, and how far I would go in building Your Kingdom. You already know every thought I think before I think it, every word I'm going to speak before I form it, and every action I will take before the moment arrives. Father thank You for Your patience and guidance because I know that I can be a handful at times. As I am encountering many obstacles in my life, I want to thank You now, not later, for helping me over, under, around, and through these troubled times.

I want to thank You for providing me with the thoughts and words to see me through those moments when there doesn't seem to be a solution. As You speak through me, my fear dissipates. I build my confidence in not needing to wonder if what I'm saying or doing makes sense because You are directing my paths. You never lead me astray. You never lead me into danger. So no matter what ugliness rears its head, I know that You are with me, protecting me. Thank You, Father. Amen.

SPEAK YOUR TRUTH
Say the words below and write beside them your truth. You can also use the workbook to write your responses.

- I Feel...
- I Am...
- I Believe...
- I Am Grateful For...
- I Will Improve...
- I Am Proud of Myself Because...
- I Will Stay Out of My/God's Way By...
- Today I Will Focus More on...

And Focus Less on...
Today I Will ...

GO DEEPER!

Please refer to **Day 29** in the workbook.

NOTES

Day 30: Grace

But by the grace of God I am what I am: and his grace which was bestowed on me was not in vain; but I labored more abundantly than they all: yet not I, but the grace of God which was with me.

—1 Corinthians 15:10 KJV

Although you are talented, gifted, intelligent, and hard-working—it is not by your doing. It is God's grace that makes it possible for you to do all that you do every day. Without Him, you are merely a shell. Without Him, you don't exist. Praise, honor and thank Him.

PRAYER
Father, thank You for Your grace and mercy upon my life. Thank You for empowering me to rise above every obstacle that I have and still may face. Thank You for restoring me and my future, and equipping me with the tools to build and climb to victory. Amen.

SPEAK YOUR TRUTH
Say the words below and write beside them your truth. You can also use the workbook to write your responses.

I Feel...
I Am...
I Believe...
I Am Grateful For...
I Will Improve...
I Am Proud of Myself Because...
I Will Stay Out of My/God's Way By...
Today I Will Focus More on...
And Focus Less on...
Today I Will ...

GO DEEPER!
Please refer to **Day 30** in the workbook.

NOTES

Day 31: Caring For Your Temple

What? Know you not that your body is the temple of the Holy Ghost which is in you, which you have of God, and you are not your own? For you are bought with a price: therefore glorify God in your body, and in your spirit, which are God's.

—I Corinthians 6:19-20 KJV

This is a heavy topic to approach. A weighted topic. Pun intended. You will need more than one or two minutes to read this as it is a topic that many of us avoid or procrastinate with. It's something that is costing a lot of us a great deal of strife and even our lives—and the outcomes are avoidable.

Today declare that no more will you make excuses for your mediocrity. You will own up to your reasons for aiming low. You will take responsibility for procrastinating, being lazy, and stagnant. Procrastination and laziness require work. You have to make a conscious effort to avoid doing what you need to do to be better and do better. You have to exert energy to choose to not do something. In some ways, you exert more energy than if you actually did something, anything towards accomplishing the task. You say that you want to be healthy, that you don't want to be sick or in pain, yet your lifestyle demonstrates the exact opposite. There's no way to have the health and body that you desire if you aren't investing the time and energy in achieving those goals. So you may not have one to two hours to workout. Do you have 20 to 30 minutes? Great. What can you get done in 20 to 30 minutes? A lot if you're really serious. You can break your workout down into smaller chunks. You can start with a five-minute cardio warm-up to get your body prepared to exert energy. Next, you can spend 10 minutes using weights or resistance bands. Then you can end your workout with five more minutes of cardio and light stretching.

As your strength and endurance increases, you can increase your resistance or the number of repetitions that you're doing. Then maybe you will find that you have time both in the morning and evening to workout. Or maybe on certain days you walk or jog. Other days you ride your bike or go for a swim, and other days you do interval training with resistance. The choice is yours. You also can do the same thing when it comes to the foods and beverages that you consume. You know what is toxic to your body. You know that sugar is the most addictive and toxic drug that you can consume. It is one that you have probably been addicted to most of your life, so it can be painfully difficult to kick the habit. But you know that the more that your body is poisoned by this drug the more it is weakened and vulnerable.

Just like with the workouts, you need to make small but meaningful changes in your eating habits. No one is telling you to aim at being thin or muscular. You should, however, want to be healthy and do your part to create a healthy environment for your mind and body. You should be doing your part to thrive and not suffer. Your body already has to work hard to fight off attacks from the environment where you work, live, and play. It already has to fight off attacks from yucky stuff that is trying to make it sick. It doesn't need you adding toxic junk to it. Your body doesn't need to be fighting you too! You either take care of your temple or it atrophies and gives up on you. No more excuses for eating junk in excess, not eating right, and not working out. No more excuses for not honoring God and the temple (your body) you claim to love.

Be the best that you are!

PRAYER

Father thank you for opening my eyes to see that my body as my temple does not belong to me, it's Yours. Just like my mind, spirit, and soul. Forgive me for not taking care of it as You expect. I apologize for not doing everything it takes to put only the best in it so that I may thrive off the energy. Forgive me for not keeping my body conditioned at the level of excellence that you created. Amen.

SPEAK YOUR TRUTH

Say the words below and write beside them your truth. You can also use the workbook to write your responses.

I Feel...
I Am...
I Believe...
I Am Grateful For...
I Will Improve...
I Am Proud of Myself Because...
I Will Stay Out of My/God's Way By...
Today I Will Focus More on...
And Focus Less on...
Today I Will ...

GO DEEPER!

Please refer to **Day 31** in the workbook.

NOTES

GO BEYOND: Month 1

DEEPER STUDY

This section is devoted to deeper study, reflection, and analysis as you end the month and begin your focus on next month. You may not be ready for this step at this moment. Please know that if you ever feel overwhelmed, you can return to this activity at a later date.

1. Describe your current situation. What burdens are you carrying around?
2. How are your finances? Do you have bills piling up and bill collectors calling and writing you?
3. Are you unemployed or underemployed? Are you uninsured or under-insured?
4. What health issues are you trying to deal with?
5. How is your love life? Is your relationship with your significant other strong and healthy? Or is it weak and failing? What is attacking your relationship? How?
6. What fears are keeping you up at night? What fears are distracting you throughout your day?

On a piece of paper write down your burdens. You can write them as a bulleted list, numbered list, or you can create a mind map like the one provided here.

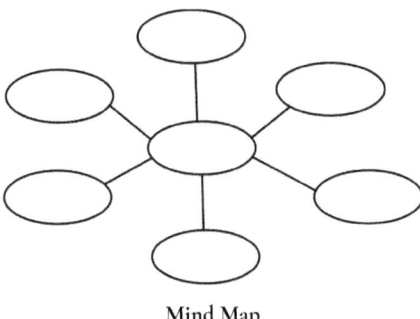

Mind Map

After writing as many burdens as you can or that you desire to list, look closely at this list. Study it. Really focus on each burden, one by one.

- Which of your burdens are financial, physical, and spiritual?
- What vessels do you have access to or can borrow that can reduce or eliminate this burden?
- What blockers do you have blinding you from seeing and embracing blessings?
- When did you turn these burdens over to God? If you haven't turned them over to Him, ask yourself why and then invest the time in answering this question.
- Are these your grievances or do you see these as merely challenges that you're charged with to overcome? Be honest with yourself. God already knows the truth. You need to face reality. If these are your grievances then identify them as such. Then identify in what ways you're responsible.
- In what ways were you not obedient? In what ways did your disobedience lead you to overlook or dismiss a blessing?
- If your burdens are physical—are you, Elisha? Or are you acting and seeing things like his servant and the Syrian army?
- Are you seeing the big picture and all the details? Or are you obsessed with the small and minute, the few and far in between?

- What has greater influence in your life, your illness, ailment, infliction, or limitation? Or God?
- Are you spiritually blind to God's presence and power? Can you not see God's Light?
- Does the false evidence of fear have a greater bearing in your life than God's proven track record?
- If you can't heal you and doctors haven't yet healed you, is there a reason why you couldn't put your faith into God's Hands? Is there a reason why you can't trust God?

What are you not seeing that God needs for you to see? Fear is the most toxic thing that you can ever ingest. It spreads as no disease can. Fear is fueled by you. It can only be destroyed when you turn your back on it and turn towards God. But it requires you to make the choice to do so and then to follow through, fully committed.

NEXT STEPS

Now, the next steps that you take are important ones. Look at your sheet of paper. Look at your burdens and fears. I want you to do something that we don't do enough—but is vital. I want you to think of at least one person (known personally by you or not) who has it worse than you. Who is in a worse financial position than you? Whose health is far worse than yours? Whose personal life is in shambles compared to yours? Take a moment and say a prayer for them. Pray for their healing restoration. Pray for their strength, courage, conviction, and faith. Pray that they never feel alone. Pray that their pain is replaced with peace. Pray that they choose joy over anger.

We can wish for and pray for better circumstances for another person. Even when we struggle to do the same thing for ourselves. We can say, "*Jeesh, I hope it gets better for Martin*" even when we can't see better for ourselves. We can visualize someone else's finish line when our lens is too clouded to see our own. We can see opportunities for others when we don't see them for ourselves. Although we may selfishly think our burdens are greater, we seem to always see solutions for others, long before we see them for ourselves. That's our pride, shame, and ego that gets in the way. Today we're going to flip our pride on its head, and we're going to put our ego on time-out. After you say your prayer for this person, I want you to do the following:

1. Find an empty shoebox, storage bag, plastic container, or coffee can that you are not using for anything else.
2. Place a label or write directly on it the words: FOR GOD
3. When you are confident in God's ability to handle and resolve your burdens, proceed to the next step below. When you are confident in His ability to provide you with opportunities and help you to see how to embrace them, proceed to the next step below. When you are confident in your ability to listen and hear more, see and identify clearly, and try your best to act through obedience—then and only then do I want you to proceed to the next step below.
4. Take this paper of burdens, fold it up, and place it inside of your FOR GOD box/envelope/bag/container.

Do NOT do this activity just to be doing it. It's then worthless. You're then just going through the motions. This step is for those of you who are ready to let go and release burdens to God.

Warning: This is not for those of you who just like to say that you're "*Letting go and letting God*". This is turning into a cliche for so many Christians. We say it just to continue stressing and crying over the same things. People love tossing around catchphrases. Church folk love call and response. We become intoxicated by the pomp and ceremony, by the traditions and fads. Let go or don't, but don't play around with this activity. This is a bold declaration for and about yourself. You're saying that you don't want to keep carrying around the weight of things that you can't change or fix. So you're releasing the burden to God.

Once you complete step three take the container and place it somewhere where you will have access. You need easy access to it so that you can add any other burdens that you want to turn over to God. You also will access it to cross off the burdens that God resolves through your faith. When a burden has been lifted, cross it off, and put the date next to it. It will serve as a constant reminder whenever fear and doubt want to rear their ugly heads.

Note: You may not be ready for the FOR GOD stage right now. Just bookmark this section and return to it when you're ready. God is patient. He will wait.

NOTES

MONTH TWO

Look Within

"They are a nation without common sense, utterly lacking in discernment. If they were wise they could figure it out and understand their destiny..."

—PARASHAH 53: HA'AZINU (HEAR) 32:28-29

[DEUTERONOMY 32: 28-29]

What possibilities and opportunities await you this month?

PONDER THIS: Month 2

"This too shall pass" is a quote that many Christians say to each other during times of struggle, pain, grief, and loss. We attribute it to scripture as highlighted in the Bible. Pastors and ministers preach sermons where they use this saying. What were you told or taught about this phrase? You may be surprised at what you will discover next, when you read **Consider This: Month 2**, located towards the back of the book.

Day 32: Forgiveness

"For if you will forgive men their offences, your Heavenly Father will forgive you also your offences. But if you will not forgive men, neither will your Father forgive you your offences."

-St Matthew 6:14-15 DRC1752

Carrying around the anger and resentment from what someone did to you will only make their issues your own. That is dead weight that you don't need in your life. That is time you are wasting fixated on them. If you really thought about it, they most likely are so far removed from that situation, that it is no longer of concern to them. Some may not even remember the incident or simply don't care. If we say that God takes care of our battles, then why don't we release them to Him and allow Him to handle our grievances? We must let go and free ourselves from that darkness.

We must forgive and move on. Honestly, can you expect something you're not willing to give in return? Can you expect forgiveness from God when you're holding grudges, causing havoc, and seeking revenge? Let the healing begin, starting today. First, you must forgive yourself for carrying around this added burden. Then you must take the next step to begin forgiving those who hurt you. It's a new day. You are blessed to be living, breathing, blinking, and thinking. Enjoy your day and your abundance of blessings.

PRAYER

Father, I pray for Your forgiveness. I am working at freeing myself by forgiving others who have sinned against me. I no longer want to carry around the dead weight from a cold heart and a closed mind. I know that I can't ask for and expect forgiveness from You if I can't find it in my heart to forgive Your children. I also know that I'm not free from blame. I've harmed someone either through my words or actions, or both. I've harmed myself by the words that I speak about myself and by not taking care of my body as I should. I need to forgive myself for the harm that I've caused others and myself. I want to be free of the guilt, insecurity, and shame that I carry. Show me how to forgive as You do. In Your name—the great I Am—I humbly pray. Amen.

SPEAK YOUR TRUTH

Say the words below and write beside them your truth. You can also use the workbook to write your responses.

> I Feel...
> I Am...
> I Believe...
> I Am Grateful For...
> I Will Improve...
> I Am Proud of Myself Because...
> I Will Stay Out of My/God's Way By...
> Today I Will Focus More on...
> And Focus Less on...
> Today I Will ...

GO DEEPER!

When you are ready to go deeper, please refer to **Day 32** in the workbook, **Seek Him: Workbook 1**. It is tied to today's theme and will help you to go farther in your exploration. Each day encourages and challenges you. Each month is more intense. Information on where to purchase the workbook is provided at end of this book.

NOTES

Day 33: God's Will

And God said, Let there be light: and there was light.

—Genesis 1:3 KJV

God speaks and there is action. God thinks and things appear or disappear. God's will is absolute. There is no confusion or need for clarity. It is pure and untarnished. God's decision in our lives is never based on misinformation or indecision. This is beyond amazing. Celebration, every single day is the least that we should do. My dear friend, Kenya Ware, forwarded me this text message years ago, "God came and spoke these words to me, "Praise will confuse the enemy"." This is absolutely true. Stay prayed up and praise our Father for all that He's done and will do in your life. When you're more focused on praising instead of complaining, the enemy has no room or time to jump in and attack you. Let's stop leaving ourselves open to attack in our daily battles in this huge war. Control your mind and your tongue, and focus on God. Are you with me?

PRAYER
Father, thank You for Your goodness and faithfulness. When I falter You don't skip a beat, You're always there. Thank You for the power in Your Word to change the world. I will align with Your plan and declare that Your will be done in my life. Thank you for being my light. Amen.

SPEAK YOUR TRUTH

Say the words below and write beside them your truth. You can also use the workbook to write your responses.

I Feel...
I Am...
I Believe...
I Am Grateful For...
I Will Improve...
I Am Proud of Myself Because...
I Will Stay Out of My/God's Way By...
Today I Will Focus More on...
And Focus Less on...
Today I Will ...

GO DEEPER!

Please refer to **Day 33** in the workbook, **Seek Him: Workbook 1**.

NOTES

Day 34: Stare Down Your Mountains

"Who art thou, O great mountain? before Zerubbabel thou dost become a plain; and he shall bring forth the head-stone with shoutings: Grace, grace unto it!"

-Zechariah 4:7 DARBY

God turns mountains into molehills. He can turn our gigantic problems into nothingness. Another name for grace is favor. When we believe in God all of the time, not just some of the time, our confidence grows. When we look at that mountain and know that God is bigger than all mountains and all things, then we realize that our problems are only big in our small, human minds.

God had a solution long before we recognized we had a problem. When I'm faced with a hiccup or misstep in life, I feel the "liar" trying to climb on my shoulders and whisper in my ear, "It's time to panic Natasha." What I'm learning to do, through courage and faith, is to breathe, staring at that mountain of chaos, and say, "I refuse to worry about you. I refuse to lose sleep over you. God is my solution, and He always has my back."

From that point, when thoughts try to creep in and distract me, I can block them out and think only of God's grace, and how great I will feel watching that mountain crumble to the ground, into a thin sheet of dirt. Let us look at our "mountains" today and this week, and stare and pray them down into absolute nothingness! Have a wonderful day, and wake up refreshed tomorrow, ready to spread God's Word and share how great He is in your life.

PRAYER

Father, thank You. Nothing and no one is greater than You, and You show me this every single day. Some days I'm in total awe of Your greatness, and other days when I've given up, and my faith wanes, I don't always acknowledge Your grace. Father forgive me. Fill me with Your love and grace so that I can conquer my mountains. Help me to believe unconditionally all of my days, not just some days. Amen.

SPEAK YOUR TRUTH

Say the words below and write beside them your truth. You can also use the workbook to write your responses.

I Feel...
I Am...
I Believe...
I Am Grateful For...
I Will Improve...
I Am Proud of Myself Because...
I Will Stay Out of My/God's Way By...
Today I Will Focus More on...
And Focus Less on...
Today I Will ...

GO DEEPER!

Please refer to **Day 34** in the workbook.

NOTES

Day 35: Putting God First

But seek ye first the kingdom of God, and his righteousness; and all these things shall be added unto you.

—Matthew 6:33 KJV

No matter what life brings or how others treat you, seek God first, and always. Push past the feelings of doubt, hesitation, fear, frustration, and anger. Reach inside—for the goodness that only God can create, provide, and replenish. This has nothing to do with others, and everything to do with you. The most important part of healing is adjusting your thinking first. You must believe that you are whole and complete and that as God's child you are free from any sickness or disease. Your mind is more powerful than your body ever could be. The next step is to watch as the part of you that wasn't aligned properly, begins to heal and become whole. We either believe in God or we don't. I believe and I seek Him. How about you?

PRAYER
Father, thank You for today, for my gift of life and health. Today, I pray for more patience and understanding. I pray that I am slow to anger or get frustrated and that I carry myself with dignity and grace in all circumstances. I strive to do better and pray that as a result I am blessed more. I seek You and I pray to seek You always. Amen.

SPEAK YOUR TRUTH

Say the words below and write beside them your truth. You can also use the workbook to write your responses.

I Feel...
I Am...
I Believe...
I Am Grateful For...
I Will Improve...
I Am Proud of Myself Because...
I Will Stay Out of My/God's Way By...
Today I Will Focus More on...
And Focus Less on...
Today I Will ...

GO DEEPER!

Please refer to **Day 35** in the workbook.

NOTES

Day 36: Celebrate Life

Though the fig tree does not bud and there is no fruit on the vines, though the olive crop fails and the fields produce no food, though there are no sheep in the pen and no cattle in the stalls, yet I will triumph in Yahweh; I will rejoice in the God of my salvation!

—Habakkuk 3:17-18 HCSB

No matter what you go through, no matter how much money and resources that you have (or have lost), no matter your health or lifestyle—celebrate your life and thank God for it. Even if you are facing the roughest moments in your life, you are alive. That means you have an opportunity to rebound and recover. Lift your hands high in the air, smile, and say, *"Thank You, Father!"* Now get out there and have an amazing day!

PRAYER

Father, I know that no matter what my situation or circumstance, You are my God and You are with me. I celebrate my life. I celebrate these experiences. I celebrate what I have with and in You. I praise Your holy Name—the great I Am. Amen.

SPEAK YOUR TRUTH

Say the words below and write beside them your truth. You can also use the workbook to write your responses.

I Feel...
I Am...
I Believe...
I Am Grateful For...
I Will Improve...
I Am Proud of Myself Because...
I Will Stay Out of My/God's Way By...
Today I Will Focus More on...
And Focus Less on...
Today I Will ...

GO DEEPER!

Please refer to **Day 36** in the workbook.

NOTES

Day 37: Elders Are Pillars

"Likewise, ye younger, submit yourselves unto the elder. Yea, all of you be subject one to another, and be clothed with humility: for God resisteth the proud, and giveth grace to the humble."

—1 Peter 5:5 KJV

Society used to respect our elders. Now we see them as taking up needed space. We are at a time where disrespect is evident and a mindset of superiority blinds us. God tells us to honor our elders for they are vessels of deep wisdom, while the youth drown in shallowness. To be free we must humble ourselves. To be humble we must let go of our personal ideals and take ahold of God's. We must strip ourselves of the layers we created and return to our rawest and purest forms. It's a new day, enjoy every second!

PRAYER
Father, remove the pride in me that holds me back. The pride that discourages me from asking for help. The pride that restricts me from giving my all in every situation and in every relationship. Father, let me continue to see my elders as the pillars that hold up Your foundation. Let my humility ground me, Lord. In Your name, I pray. Amen.

SPEAK YOUR TRUTH

Say the words below and write beside them your truth. You can also use the workbook to write your responses.

I Feel...
I Am...
I Believe...
I Am Grateful For...
I Will Improve...
I Am Proud of Myself Because...
I Will Stay Out of My/God's Way By...
Today I Will Focus More on...
And Focus Less on...
Today I Will ...

GO DEEPER!

Please refer to **Day 37** in the workbook.

NOTES

Day 38: Stop Resisting

For it were better for them not to have known the way of righteousness, than, after knowing it, to turn back from the holy commandment delivered unto them.

—2 Peter 2:21 KJV

God sent us His Son so that we may know Him. Many of us still don't see the correlation, still don't study God's Word, or follow Jesus' examples. This message is really for those of us who have grown up in churches. Those of us with a long history with the religious foundation, symbolism, and culture. We can quote, share parables, and pretend that we truly understand and embrace our walk. We can make bumper stickers and calendars, write books, preach and teach, and give speeches. All while living unrighteously.

We need to stop being hypocrites and start living the lives that God put us here to lead. We need to stop misleading others with our lies and deceit. We need to stop being selfish and start being selfless, putting others' needs first before our own. We need to think of how we can best serve others rather than how we can best benefit from the equation. We need to focus intently on putting God and Jesus first before all others. Our days should begin, end, and be filled with prayers, thoughts, and thanks to God and Jesus. Some people feel that they are gods because they are rulers and leaders of governments and organizations. But God has a special treat in store for them! There is none greater than our Father. If you continue to:

- Resist change,
- Resist God's molding hands,
- Resist those people that God placed in your life to make you a better person, and,
- Resist doing things that feel uncomfortable to you—although they serve God's plan

Then you were better off not knowing the way to righteousness. Instead of only keeping track of the good things that you do, stop from time-to-time and take note of what you don't do, didn't do, and won't do. Who do you refuse to listen to? Who did you hurt simply because you could? Who didn't you love fully? Who did you neglect and ignore? If you don't have time for God's children how can you say that you are devoted and have time for Him? If what you didn't do outweighs what you have done in life, then the good deeds that you have done have been for naught. Just think about it.

PRAYER
Father, I don't want to make a mockery of Your holy name, and of Your goodness and kindness. I don't want to make a mockery of those before me that You sent to spread Your Word and build Your Kingdom. Before I speak let me pray to You for Your words to flow through me. As I listen to your children, let me listen for Your voice as a filter. Let me see that everything in life is about You, not me, not the people I know or anyone else.

The sun rises and the moon grows full because of You Father. Winds blow, water flows, flowers bloom, and stars twinkle because of You. Thank You, Father, for another day, another breath, my blinking eyes, and beating heart. Thank You, Father, for my mind that I might reason, and make decisions to live righteously or not. Thank You for all of my experiences, the good and the not so pleasant. They have taught me so much about myself, about You, and about my purpose. In Your name, I pray. Amen.

SPEAK YOUR TRUTH

Say the words below and write beside them your truth. You can also use the workbook to write your responses.

I Feel...
I Am...
I Believe...
I Am Grateful For...
I Will Improve...
I Am Proud of Myself Because...
I Will Stay Out of My/God's Way By...
Today I Will Focus More on...
And Focus Less on...
Today I Will ...

GO DEEPER!

Please refer to **Day 38** in the workbook.

NOTES

Day 39: Fear

If you fully obey the lord your God and carefully follow His commands...you will be blessed in the city and blessed in the country.

—Deuteronomy 28:1-3 NIV

In August 2010, I was in the ocean scuba diving. I had two minor mishaps that normally would have made me get out of the water pronto. I stayed in. I went under several feet. Something happened and when the fear kicked in I didn't have faith that God's hand was protecting me. I got back in the boat. Fear conquered me. Now I gotta try again, to remind myself to Whom I belong, and that fear does not belong to (or in) me. Don't let fear keep you from expressing and demonstrating who you are and what you're made of. Don't let fear keep you from your blessings!

PRAYER
Father, thank You for the many blessings that You have bestowed upon me. I choose today to put You first in everything that I do. To overcome my fears and increase my confidence I must see myself and my situations as You do. Perfect in Your eyes with no mistakes. And always protected and cared for. Help me to walk in integrity and humility. Help me to follow your commands so that I may honor You always and be blessed no matter where I go in life. Amen.

SPEAK YOUR TRUTH

Say the words below and write beside them your truth. You can also use the workbook to write your responses.

I Feel...
I Am...
I Believe...
I Am Grateful For...
I Will Improve...
I Am Proud of Myself Because...
I Will Stay Out of My/God's Way By...
Today I Will Focus More on...
And Focus Less on...
Today I Will...

GO DEEPER!

Please refer to **Day 39** in the workbook.

NOTES

Day 40: Servant Leaders vs. Self-Serving

The greatest among you must be a servant. But those who exalt themselves will be humbled, and those who humble themselves will be exalted.

—Matthew 23:11-12 NLT

There is no human too great to serve others. There is no one higher or more powerful than God. Those who stand before God's flock and speak as though they are equal to God will be humbled. Those who claim to be the only way in which to gain God's glory will be humbled quickly by Him. No religious leader can place themselves on a pedestal and think God won't knock them down. These people are here to serve God and to serve us, not the other way around.

We have a lot of people walking and strutting around with God and Messiah complexes. One day, they have to answer to God and explain why they misrepresented themselves to the children of God. It's difficult to justify living a lifestyle that you earned off of the blood, sweat, and tears of others. Especially when those people are living in poverty. So think twice before jumping to raise money to buy Pastor a new Bentley. What purpose does that really serve? How will that get you closer to God? How will that etch out your footing in Heaven? How will that atone for your sins? Just think about it!

PRAYER
Father, I serve You and Your children with great honor and humility. I thank You for my blessings. I thank You for the privilege to serve and be of service. Show me more ways I can best serve as Your ambassador. In Your name, I pray. Amen.

SPEAK YOUR TRUTH
Say the words below and write beside them your truth. You can also use the workbook to write your responses.

- I Feel...
- I Am...
- I Believe...
- I Am Grateful For...
- I Will Improve...
- I Am Proud of Myself Because...
- I Will Stay Out of My/God's Way By...
- Today I Will Focus More on...
- And Focus Less on...
- Today I Will ...

GO DEEPER!
Please refer to **Day 40** in the workbook.

NOTES

Day 41: Recklessness

Reckless words pierce like a sword, but the tongue of the wise brings healing.

—Proverbs 12:18 NIV

Focus on the here and now. Focus on praying before speaking. Clear your negative thoughts and pray that they are replaced by pure, loving ones. So that they might uplift and heal, rather than tear down and destroy. What we say can be just as or more harmful to ourselves and others as what we do. Protect your mind and heart from recklessness in thought, speech, and deed. Understand that even if you're speaking the truth it's gossip.

If you're not part of the solution, then you're part of the problem. If you're gossiping about them but not working directly with them, then you're part of the problem. Be silent. We're so quick to talk about everyone's business. How would we feel hearing that people who claimed to be friends and loved ones were gossiping about us? How would we feel if the very person who came to help us was turning around and gossiping about us? Doesn't sound that great and entertaining when put that way, does it? Let's stop being reckless!

PRAYER

Father, today I choose to be wise and bring healing to myself and others with my words. I ask for more patience, tolerance, love, care, and consideration. I ask for more respect and wisdom so that I may honor and reflect you. Amen.

SPEAK YOUR TRUTH

Say the words below and write beside them your truth. You can also use the workbook to write your responses.

- I Feel…
- I Am…
- I Believe…
- I Am Grateful For…
- I Will Improve…
- I Am Proud of Myself Because…
- I Will Stay Out of My/God's Way By…
- Today I Will Focus More on…
- And Focus Less on…
- Today I Will …

GO DEEPER!

Please refer to **Day 41** in the workbook.

NOTES

Day 42: Watch Your Words

What goes into a man's mouth does not make him 'unclean,' but what comes out of his mouth, that is what makes him 'unclean....

Don't you see that whatever enters the mouth goes into the stomach and then out of the body? But the things that come out of the mouth come from the heart, and these make a man 'unclean.' For out of the heart come evil thoughts, murder, adultery, sexual immorality, theft, false testimony, slander. These are what make a man 'unclean'....

—Matthew 15:11, 17-20 NIV

We must watch what we say to and about ourselves, and to (and about) others. We must take responsibility for our part in our interactions with others. We can't merely say, *"That's their problem"* because their problem can soon become our problem. We must always be prayerful. We must immediately change our thinking when something negative seeps in. We must say to the enemy, *"You are a liar"* and force the negativity out. We must not allow our hearts to be misled. If our focus is on God, and we pray to Him constantly throughout our day—then we can tell the difference between something of God and of the world. We can tell the difference between God's voice and His light. And that of our mortal mind, which is clouded and fractured. Before we say or do something, let's first stop and think about God. Think about whether we'd do and say this in front of His Son, Jesus. If you have to think about it, then You know you're about to be on a slippery slope of foolishness. Stop and walk away. If you haven't grown in your relationship with God and Jesus, read this:

Ask yourself if you would do or say this in public? Or in front of your closest family members? Your children? Your boss, co-workers or employees? Would you want what you did or said put on the Internet and on every television news station? Would you want to see it in the newspapers? If the answer is no, then walk away and don't do it. Don't send the compromising picture, letter, card, email or text message. Don't make that phone call or leave that voicemail. Don't angrily drive over to someone's home or workplace to confront them. If you wouldn't want to explain yourself and your actions afterward, then opt to not do it. Our 'dirt' has a way of slamming us in the face when we least expect it! We can never take back something we have said or done. When put that way, it may seem more simple to comprehend. God wants you to do right, to live right, and to represent Him the right way.

So whatever positive and righteous methods you need to take to do this, then do it. I needed to read this scripture I shared today. I simply turned to it and my eyes saw the passages, and I began to type as I prayed and reflected on the verses. Maybe this message was meant for you, maybe someone you know may benefit from reading it. I don't know. I simply share what flows through me. One day it may be a short message, and then there are days like today where I pray and reflect until everything is said. It's a new day—make the most of it and stay prayed up!

PRAYER

Father, being from You and not of the world I know that all that I need can only come from You. No man can protect, provide, and bring purpose to my life—only You can do that Father. Protect me, Lord. Protect me from me. Protect me from allowing others' fears to seep inside of me where I lose my focus on You. Protect my heart, Lord. Protect it from desiring the instant gratifica-

tion the world provides. Protect it from harm, from those who would want to control it and my mind. Protect me from buying into the lies that others tell. Protect me from telling lies to myself and others.

Provide me with words of truth, even if that truth causes temporary pain. Provide me with the words to heal and with the courage to walk away from anything or anyone that is not in Your Light. Show me my purpose, Father. Show me the path, even when I veer off in another direction. Show me how I can be the best ambassador that I can be.

Show me how to avoid falling into the trappings of this world, how to say no to temptation, and how to turn my head and my heart away from the yearnings of the flesh. Show me the real intent of those who surround me. Show me how to remain focused on Your plan for me, and not be seduced by dreams and desires for instant gratification. Reveal to me the wolf in sheep's clothing and the seducer only out for self. Reveal the manipulator who is around to cause havoc and gleam in victory. I thank You Father for all that You do, even when I mess up. In Jesus' name, I pray. Amen.

SPEAK YOUR TRUTH

Say the words below and write beside them your truth. You can also use the workbook to write your responses.

> I Feel…
> I Am…
> I Believe…
> I Am Grateful For…
> I Will Improve…
> I Am Proud of Myself Because…
> I Will Stay Out of My/God's Way By…
> Today I Will Focus More on…
> And Focus Less on…
> Today I Will …

GO DEEPER!

Please refer to **Day 42** in the workbook.

NOTES

Day 43: Testify to God's Greatness

Behold, the Lord God will come with strong hand, and his arm shall rule for him: behold, his reward is with him, and his work before him. He shall feed his flock like a shepherd: he shall gather the lambs with his arm, and carry them in his bosom, and shall gently lead those that are with young.

—Isaiah 40:10-11 KJV

Free yourself from your self. Breathe deeply as you allow God to direct, lead, correct, encourage, and nurture you. God is good ALL of the time, even in rough times! Stand up and testify to this!

PRAYER
Father, You are both great and good, just and loving, protecting, and nurturing. You are always there for me even in my darkest hour. I embrace Your strong hand as You guide me and correct my steps. I will turn to You both in good times and in bad as my answer and encourager. When I stray please turn me right so that I may be on Your path on Your timetable. Amen.

SPEAK YOUR TRUTH

Say the words below and write beside them your truth. You can also use the workbook to write your responses.

I Feel...
I Am...
I Believe...
I Am Grateful For...
I Will Improve...
I Am Proud of Myself Because...
I Will Stay Out of My/God's Way By...
Today I Will Focus More on...
And Focus Less on...
Today I Will ...

GO DEEPER!

Please refer to **Day 43** in the workbook.

NOTES

Day 44: Our Choices

Grace to you and peace be multiplied in the knowledge of God and of Jesus our Lord; whereby he hath granted unto us his precious and exceeding great promises; seeing that his divine power hath granted unto us all things that pertain unto life and godliness, through the knowledge of him that called us by his own glory and virtue; that through these ye may become partakers of the divine nature, having escaped from the corruption that is in that world by lust. Yea, and for this very cause adding on your part all diligence, in your faith supply virtue; and in your virtue knowledge; and in your knowledge self-control; and in your self-control patience; and in your patience godliness; and in your godliness brotherly kindness; and in your brotherly kindness love. For if these things are yours and abound, they make you to be not idle nor unfruitful unto the knowledge of our Lord Jesus Christ. For he that lacketh these things is blind, seeing only what is near, having forgotten the cleansing from his old sins. Wherefore, brethren, give the more diligence to make your calling and election sure: for if ye do these things, ye shall never stumble: for thus shall be richly supplied unto you the entrance into the eternal kingdom of our Lord and Saviour Jesus Christ. Wherefore I shall be ready always to put you in remembrance of these things, though ye know them, and are established in the truth which is with you.

—2 Peter 1:2-12 ASV

We know what is right and wrong. But we all need constant reminders of what is expected of us and our roles if we are to be a part of God's Kingdom. We must change starting right now. None of us are perfect. Every day we should work at being better children. More patient, loving, nurturing, forgiving, and understanding. We should correct ourselves when we judge others, expect people to conform to our wants and needs, and when we don't place God first in our decisions. We are to conform only to God. So check yourself if you have forgotten your primary position as His child and follower. No one should ever place another human, animal, or object before the Lord. All decisions should be made on what He says. And what His son, Jesus Christ, would say and do if you asked him for advice and direction. There is only one way. You must choose to be God-centered or ego-centered. Which will you choose?

PRAYER

To know You is to love You, Lord. I have not forgotten the sins I have been cleansed of. Nor have I forgotten the sins that I have recently committed. Remind me of my role, my purpose, my commitments, and of Your expectations Father. So that I may come to a place in my life where I won't stumble and fall, but see clearly what lies ahead, and make the right decisions. Thank You for your loving guidance, Your angels that protect me and show me the way, and for Your son who is the ultimate example. I love You Father. Amen.

SPEAK YOUR TRUTH

Say the words below and write beside them your truth. You can also use the workbook to write your responses.

- I Feel...
- I Am...
- I Believe...
- I Am Grateful For...
- I Will Improve...
- I Am Proud of Myself Because...

I Will Stay Out of My/God's Way By...
Today I Will Focus More on...
And Focus Less on...
Today I Will ...

GO DEEPER!

Please refer to **Day 44** in the workbook.

NOTES

Day 45: Nobody Has Your Back Like God Does

"Yahweh your God is among you, a warrior who saves. He will rejoice over you with gladness. He will bring you quietness with His love. He will delight in you with shouts of joy."

—Zephaniah 3:17 HCSB

No friend or family member could ever have your back or love you as God does. No one can ever provide for you spiritually, emotionally, or financially as God can. Doesn't the thought of that bring a smile to your face? Now, what will you do with this information? Will you walk in doubt or in faith?

PRAYER
Thank You for being a loving, just, caring, and protecting Father. As I walk on my journey through life I know that You will always be here watching, waiting, and looking over me. In Jesus' name, I humbly pray to You. Amen.

SPEAK YOUR TRUTH
Say the words below and write beside them your truth. You can also use the workbook to write your responses.

I Feel...
I Am...
I Believe...
I Am Grateful For...
I Will Improve...
I Am Proud of Myself Because...
I Will Stay Out of My/God's Way By...
Today I Will Focus More on...
And Focus Less on...
Today I Will ...

GO DEEPER!
Please refer to **Day 45** in the workbook.

NOTES

Day 46: LOVE

This is a trustworthy saying, and everyone should accept it: "Christ Jesus came into the world to save sinners"—and I am the worst of them all. But God had mercy on me so that Christ Jesus could use me as a prime example of his great patience with even the worst sinners. Then others will realize that they, too, can believe in him and receive eternal life. All honor and glory to God forever and ever! He is the eternal King, the unseen one who never dies; he alone is God. Amen.

—1 Timothy 1:15 NLT

If one of the worst sinners turned out to be one of the most loyal and committed servants then there's hope for all of us. His testimony proves that God can change any person, heal the most difficult, raise the most stubborn, and realign the broken. Our minor does not compare to his major and look what God did for him. Imagine what God has devised for you. Be inspired and optimistic about what awaits you. While you wait, continue to help others in service of our Heavenly Father. Just as our Savior Jesus Christ led through example. As you humbly bless others, without concern for recognition and praise, God will bless you with abundance. He will keep your cup full of reserves and running over.

PRAYER

Thank You, Father, for loving me. Thank You for Your grace and mercy that rose me another day. I'm fully functional, and ready to learn and experience all that I need to be a better child, servant, follower, believer, and student. Thank You for the constant reminders of the power of faith, optimism, and God-confidence. I thank You for all that You have done, all that You're currently doing, and all that You will do. In Jesus' name, I praise You. Amen.

SPEAK YOUR TRUTH

Say the words below and write beside them your truth. You can also use the workbook to write your responses.

> I Feel…
> I Am…
> I Believe…
> I Am Grateful For…
> I Will Improve…
> I Am Proud of Myself Because…
> I Will Stay Out of My/God's Way By…
> Today I Will Focus More on…
> And Focus Less on…
> Today I Will …

GO DEEPER!

Please refer to **Day 46** in the workbook.

NOTES

Day 47: Free From The Law of Sin & Death

For the law of the Spirit of life in Christ Jesus hath made me free from the law of sin and death. For what the law could not do, in that it was weak through the flesh, God sending his own Son in the likeness of sinful flesh, and for sin, condemned sin in the flesh: That the righteousness of the law might be fulfilled in us, who walk not after the flesh, but after the Spirit.

—Romans 8:2-4 KJV

God sent Jesus to prove in the "flesh" that man's laws and thinking would always be dwarfed by God. That man's mind was limited in capability and power compared to Mind (God's). Jesus did the will of our Father and proved that man's devices and authority was false. He healed sickness and disease through God's law of Spirit, never turning to man's law of medicine. He even showed his disciples how to heal. That meant that regular Joe Blow, the farmer was healing people through Jesus' teachings and guidance. This proves the power of Mind. It proves God's law of life.

God sent Jesus to prove that we are spiritual beings having a human experience and not the other way around. That is why after his resurrection something was different about him. He had transformed. He was no longer limited and bound in and of the flesh. He reached the level many of us wish to achieve one day. As long as we continue to put man's laws before God, remain rigid in our thinking, and constrained by the flesh, we will never get there. Ponder that.

PRAYER

Father, You have sent countless servants to show us the way and Your Truth. You sent Jesus to make us see, to show us how, to prove what we can do, and to show that we give power to darkness when we give in to the flesh. You have proven to us the limited reality of our human flesh and the lie that we keep buying about who we are. Father, forgive us for choosing man's laws over Yours. Forgive us for buying into a man-made story for our lives.

There is no greater than You. No truth but Yours, and no better place to be than with You. Forgive me for my weakness, fear, and lack of total faith. Forgive me for not always wanting to see what awaits me in the forest. Forgive me for complaining throughout my walk. Forgive me for being fearful when You tell me to be strong. Forgive me for thinking that I'm too tired to do what You ask but then later finding the energy to do something that satisfies the flesh. I pray to be made whole in Jesus' name. Amen.

SPEAK YOUR TRUTH

Say the words below and write beside them your truth. You can also use the workbook to write your responses.

- I Feel...
- I Am...
- I Believe...
- I Am Grateful For...
- I Will Improve...
- I Am Proud of Myself Because...
- I Will Stay Out of My/God's Way By...
- Today I Will Focus More on...
- And Focus Less on...
- Today I Will ...

GO DEEPER!
Please refer to **Day** 47 in the workbook.

NOTES

Day 48: God's Provisions

And he came into all the region round about the Jordan, preaching the baptism of repentance unto remission of sins; as it is written in the book of the words of Isaiah the prophet, The voice of one crying in the wilderness, Make ye ready the way of the Lord, Make his paths straight. Every valley shall be filled, And every mountain and hill shall be brought low; And the crooked shall become straight, And the rough ways smooth; And all flesh shall see the salvation of God.

—Luke 3:3-6 ASV

Every twist and turn, bump and dip, God has the power and the grace to make all things straight, smooth, and level. When you're lost, God will show you the path out. Every day we must show our faith in Him, and His ability to meet our needs and exceed our expectations. We must thank Him for our blessings, even the ones that we haven't received yet. Think about the small things that are actually huge when you no longer have use of them. Like the sense of smell, taste, sight, hearing, and touch. Thank Him for the ones you actively have use of. Thank Him for the ones that are heightened as they make up for the ones you no longer have full use of. They are all gifts from our Father. You may not have money to pay your bills, but thank God for providing for you. Thank Him for those coins you ran across in your home, car, on the bus, or on the street. Thank Him for the gift card you forgot about, which made it possible for you to buy food, gas, or toiletries. Thank Him for touching the heart of your debt collector, who opts to accept payment arrangements with you, rather than dragging you down the debtor's path of shame. Thank Him because He does all of this out of love for you. Not obligation. Not because you deserve it.

Whatever you do, don't take for granted God's gifts to you. Don't grow an attitude of passive expectancy. You have a role in this blessing besides receiving His gifts. If you owe money to someone, don't just say, "God's got this" and then do absolutely nothing. Take the steps to contact the person you owe the debt. Make payment arrangements. Offer a good faith payment of a lower amount. Pay off the debt as more money comes in by God's favor. Our Father doesn't do laziness. You have to be a hard-working and diligent steward in His Kingdom. You can't walk around with your hand out like a spoiled child. You must work. You must push yourself to the threshold, and then keep pushing.

At the same time, God doesn't look favorably at those who show no grace to others but expect to receive it from Him. If someone owes a debt to you, show compassion. Remember those people and companies that you owe money to. What would you pray that they would do if you had difficulties paying them on time or at all? Don't forget, to receive a blessing we must be a blessing. Life is a constant cycle. What we put in it we get out of it. If you're paying your bills late, guess what? Someone is going to be late paying you.

If you make a habit of only paying a fraction of a bill, don't be surprised when your paycheck is short. Or when someone only pays part of your invoice. When you don't tip your server adequately, don't be surprised that you get mediocre service elsewhere. It is a cycle. God's always doing His part. We must do ours if we expect to see the fruits of our labor. And to be prepared for the bounty of blessings that He has planned for us. This week, focus on doing your part to make the cycle of life work not only for you but your fellow brothers and sisters. Do your part to make those crooked paths straight, to raise the deep valleys, and flatten the mountains and hills.

PRAYER

Father, I pray for my hills and mountains to be flattened to nothingness. I want to see clearly, even with obstacles in my way. I want to see through them, because they are not Your reality, so they can't possibly be mine. I'm claiming this victory, today Lord. In Jesus' name, I humbly and sincerely pray. Amen.

SPEAK YOUR TRUTH

Say the words below and write beside them your truth. You can also use the workbook to write your responses.

> I Feel...
> I Am...
> I Believe...
> I Am Grateful For...
> I Will Improve...
> I Am Proud of Myself Because...
> I Will Stay Out of My/God's Way By...
> Today I Will Focus More on...
> And Focus Less on...
> Today I Will ...

GO DEEPER!

Please refer to **Day 48** in the workbook.

NOTES

Day 49: God is Always Working

And they remembered that God was their rock, and the high God their redeemer. Nevertheless they did flatter him with their mouth, and they lied unto him with their tongues. For their heart was not right with him, neither were they stedfast in his covenant. But he, being full of compassion, forgave their iniquity, and destroyed them not: For he remembered that they were but flesh; a wind that passeth away, and cometh not again.

—Psalm 78:35-39 KJV

Even in the Old Testament, we had issues with trusting and believing in God. What must He do to prove that He's here and ALWAYS working? I can understand the Israelite struggles when I take into consideration the historical context. Let's flashback in time. When Moses helped lead them out of Egypt, he led thousands of people with various customs, beliefs, and religions. They didn't just start worshipping gods and idols once in the wilderness. They were worshipping gods and idols in Egypt. So many of them had grown accustomed to life in Egypt. They knew and abided by the laws and customs. That is why when they became frustrated with Moses, they would argue that life was better in Egypt. Because at least they knew what to expect.

They did not like the unknowns of their new life. The God of Abraham, Isaac, and Jacob (later named Israel by God) was not the God that everyone was worshipping and having a relationship with. When I look at things from that perspective I have to then say, I can sympathize with their struggle. There are people in modern days that grew up as Christians, know what is expected of us, and we struggle. That is why it is so awesome how much God loves us, to lead us through grace and not by force. That does not mean that we should slack off on our commitment and re-commitment. We should grateful for God's love and forgiveness. If only we could show that level of love and forgiveness.

PRAYER
Father, you have done so much for me. You have forgiven so many things and redirected me so many times. Yet in hard times, I doubt You, believing that my issues are mine for me to solve. Or I worry that you won't solve them fast enough. Father forgive me as you know my heart and my desire to rely solely upon you. Amen.

SPEAK YOUR TRUTH
Say the words below and write beside them your truth. You can also use the workbook to write your responses.

I Feel...
I Am...
I Believe...
I Am Grateful For...
I Will Improve...
I Am Proud of Myself Because...
I Will Stay Out of My/God's Way By...
Today I Will Focus More on...
And Focus Less on...
Today I Will ...

GO DEEPER!
Please refer to **Day 49** in the workbook.

NOTES

Day 50: Will You Reject God?

Nevertheless they would not hear, but stiffened their necks, like the necks of their fathers, who did not believe in the Lord their God. And they rejected His statutes and His covenant that He had made with their fathers, and His testimonies which He had testified against them; they followed idols, became idolaters, and went after the nations who were all around them, concerning whom the Lord had charged them that they should not do like them.

—2 Kings 17:14-15 NKJV

Will you reject Him, become vain, and think *"I can do this myself"*? Will you ignore His promises to you and your promises to Him? Will you choose to follow idols and recite their words over His? Will you assimilate to be like others, or live free through Him? Rather than focusing on what you can do or need to do, consider changing your thoughts and speech to align with, *"What do WE need to do?"* And *"How will WE handle this Father?"* Walking with God is much better than walking alone.

PRAYER

Father, warm my heart. Free my mind and loosen my neck so that I may always hear You, turn in the direction You point, and follow Your path. Thank You for Your love and patience. I have not and will not forget Your Word and promise. I'm ready to do this with you. Giving You the glory. Amen.

SPEAK YOUR TRUTH

Say the words below and write beside them your truth. You can also use the workbook to write your responses.

- I Feel...
- I Am...
- I Believe...
- I Am Grateful For...
- I Will Improve...
- I Am Proud of Myself Because...
- I Will Stay Out of My/God's Way By...
- Today I Will Focus More on...
- And Focus Less on...
- Today I Will ...

GO DEEPER!

Please refer to **Day 50** in the workbook.

NOTES

Day 51: Grace of God… Seek Him in Everything

But by the grace of God I am what I am: and his grace which was bestowed on me was not in vain; but I labored more abundantly than they all: yet not I, but the grace of God which was with me.

—1 Corinthians 15:10 KJV

Although you are talented, gifted, intelligent, and hard-working—it is not by your doing. It is God's grace that makes it possible for you to do all that you do every day. Without Him, you are merely a shell and irrelevant. Without Him, you don't exist.

Praise, honor and thank Him.

PRAYER
Father, thank You for Your grace and mercy upon my life. Thank You for empowering me to rise above every obstacle I have and still may face. Thank You for restoring me and my future, and equipping me with the tools to build and climb to victory. Amen.

SPEAK YOUR TRUTH

Say the words below and write beside them your truth. You can also use the workbook to write your responses.

I Feel...
I Am...
I Believe...
I Am Grateful For...
I Will Improve...
I Am Proud of Myself Because...
I Will Stay Out of My/God's Way By...
Today I Will Focus More on...
And Focus Less on...
Today I Will ...

GO DEEPER!

Please refer to **Day 51** in the workbook.

NOTES

Day 52: Your Heart

In that night did God appear unto Solomon, and said unto him, Ask what I shall give thee. And Solomon said unto God, Thou hast shewed great mercy unto David my father, and hast made me to reign in his stead. Give me now wisdom and knowledge, that I may go out and come in before this people: for who can judge this thy people, that is so great?

And God said to Solomon, Because this was in thine heart, and thou hast not asked riches, wealth, or honour, nor the life of thine enemies, neither yet hast asked long life; but hast asked wisdom and knowledge for thyself, that thou mayest judge my people, over whom I have made thee king: Wisdom and knowledge is granted unto thee; and I will give thee riches, and wealth, and honour, such as none of the kings have had that have been before thee, neither shall there any after thee have the like.

—2 Chronicles 1:7,8,10-12 KJV

I want you to read this again tonight so that before you go to sleep you have God on your mind and in your heart. Then, when you wake up He is the first thing that you think of to get your day started right. Tonight ask yourself what you truly need in your life. What do you need to be a better person? Pray to God for what you need to be a better ambassador. God knows what is in your heart. Your heart will always reflect your truest self. Hopefully, it also reflects our heavenly Father. Be the example you want to see in others, the example you know God expects to see consistently. Have a blessed day, prepared for new experiences. Tonight, as you rest, be prepared to begin tomorrow with a fresh start and a new outlook on life.

PRAYER
Father touch my heart that I may be as humble as Solomon. Bless me, Lord, with what I need to be a better ambassador for You and Your Kingdom. I thank You now for Your blessings. Amen.

SPEAK YOUR TRUTH
Say the words below and write beside them your truth. You can also use the workbook to write your responses.

- I Feel...
- I Am...
- I Believe...
- I Am Grateful For...
- I Will Improve...
- I Am Proud of Myself Because...
- I Will Stay Out of My/God's Way By...
- Today I Will Focus More on...
- And Focus Less on...
- Today I Will ...

GO DEEPER!
Please refer to **Day 52** in the workbook.

NOTES

Day 53: There is No Hiding The Truth

This is the message which we have heard from Him and declare to you, that God is light and in Him is no darkness at all. If we say that we have fellowship with Him, and walk in darkness, we lie and do not practice the truth. But if we walk in the light as He is in the light, we have fellowship with one another, and the blood of Jesus Christ His Son cleanses us from all sin. If we say that we have no sin, we deceive ourselves, and the truth is not in us. If we confess our sins, He is faithful and just to forgive us our sins and to cleanse us from all unrighteousness. If we say that we have not sinned, we make Him a liar, and His word is not in us.

—1 John 1:5-10 NKJV

It is amazing how God works. Several years ago I had a lengthy conversation with two dear friends about marriage. We spoke about the game-playing in relationships. We discussed "ingredients" such as love, sacrifice, trust, honesty, transparency, and devotion. After the conversation, I left to run errands for a couple of hours. While I was driving I had a lot on my mind, and my heart grew heavy. My two friends shared some great stories about love and overcoming temptation. They also shared how they built a healthy relationship with God as their foundation. They knew soon after meeting their spouses that they were meant to marry them and love them for life. I reflected on what my friends had to say, and about their advice. I began to pray. I prayed for a healthy relationship and a marriage, with a man that would resist temptations and meet God's requirements for a union. I prayed that God would provide my relationship with the tools to fight anything and anyone who would attempt to interfere.

Before I got home that day, I received a disturbing dose of the harsh realities of living in and of the world. A close friend contacted me by phone. They were in a great deal of pain over a person they love deeply, and who they thought felt the same way about them. God doesn't intentionally hurt us. The truth in the light may reveal some things that hurt us because we were blindly walking in darkness. Seeing reality for the first time feels more like a dream state. It can feel like a nightmare. Without sharing all the details of my friend's sad story, I will share the root of their issues. Then I will reconnect it to today's scripture.

This friend had been feeling weary about their loved one for several weeks. They had been prayerful and asking God to reveal the truth about this other person. They wanted to know their honest intentions and whether this relationship was for a reason, a season, or a lifetime. Gradually 'bread crumbs' of truth had lined a path that was revealing a reality far from the dreamland my friend was living in for almost a year. Notes, cards, and other correspondence from so-called "friends" had surfaced. They noted the phone calls at awkward times of the day and night. The conversations sounded strained and awkward.

There were other irregular behaviors that had sent up red flags. My friend had naively been labeling these flags as their own jealousy and insecurity. They had been in denial. So-called "friends" were turning out to be much more. This relationship that seemed to have been built on truth, love, and respect, was crashing. Because it was built on lies, deceit, selfishness, and fear. Simply put, sin was eating away at their relationship. My friend was asking God what they did to deserve this; why they had to be subjected to this pain and embarrassment. They had so many questions that they wanted answers to.

We always deserve the truth. We always deserve to have God point us in the right direction and let us know when we're going in the wrong direction. We need to know when the wrong people are in our lives to lead us astray. It is the light within us that makes another person led by the "liar" to deceive, manipulate, and hurt us. The "liar" has hopes of drowning out that light with darkness. The "liar" has one goal, and that is to keep you from the truth, to keep you in the dark- oblivious, ignorant, and lonely. Even when you're not alone. You can't control what someone else does, says, or thinks. But you can walk away from their darkness, and step into God's light.

You have choices in life. You can freely sin and walk in darkness, content with being misled. As long as it makes you feel complete having someone by you that falsely claims to love you. Or you can walk upright, with your head and heart in the right direction- pointing towards God and His son. We pray for the truth. We pray for enlightenment. God always delivers. We may not like what is revealed, but it is better to walk in the light of truth than in the deception of darkness.

PRAYER

Father, there is no hiding the truth from You. I have sinned many times in my life. I even sinned today. You saw me sin. You heard me sin. You knew I was going to do it. I knew You would know, but I did it anyway. Father forgive me. In my moments of weakness, I listen to the "liar" who says, "No one will know. Do it this one time." But I forget that You and Your son always know. Instead of turning to the light for strength, I hide my face in shame in the darkness. Cleanse me, Father. Turn my heart towards You when I am seduced by the "liar" to do wrong.

Turn my eyes to focus on You and where I'm supposed to be. Let me not lose focus when my attention is caught by something or someone unrighteous. Father also please forgive me for deceiving your children I claim to love. When I say one thing yet do another, let me see the err of my ways immediately that I may correct my missteps. Help me to be open, honest, and sincere in my dealings with all people. Steer me away from playing games with people's hearts and lives. Humble me, Father. In Your Kingdom, there is no room for my selfish lifestyle and behavior. *I want to live righteously Father. In Your son's name, I pray. Amen.*

SPEAK YOUR TRUTH

Say the words below and write beside them your truth. You can also use the workbook to write your responses.

I Feel...
I Am...
I Believe...
I Am Grateful For...
I Will Improve...
I Am Proud of Myself Because...
I Will Stay Out of My/God's Way By...
Today I Will Focus More on...
And Focus Less on...
Today I Will ...

GO DEEPER!

Please refer to **Day 53** in the workbook.

NOTES

Day 54: Getting Aligned

The instruction of the Lord is perfect, renewing one's life; the testimony of the Lord is trustworthy, making the inexperienced wise. The precepts of the Lord are right, making the heart glad; the command of the Lord is radiant, making the eyes light up.

—Psalms 19:7-8 HCSB

The words *perfect, sure, whole, complete,* and *right* **all** define God and our relationship with Him. Opposite of these are not of God, so they can't be a part of us. Be aligned in and with Him. Your judgment and the judgment of others is not necessary. God's judgment is prevailing and always correct. We are not perfect, sure, whole, complete, and right if we are not of and obedient to God.

PRAYER
Your law, commands, and guidance are all that I need. Align me, Father. Provide me with vision and the clarity to see clearly. And the wisdom and discernment to know Your voice above all others. So that I may do right and live right—by Your eyes. Thank You, Lord.

SPEAK YOUR TRUTH
Say the words below and write beside them your truth. You can also use the workbook to write your responses.

I Feel...
I Am...
I Believe...
I Am Grateful For...
I Will Improve...
I Am Proud of Myself Because...
I Will Stay Out of My/God's Way By...
Today I Will Focus More on...
And Focus Less on...
Today I Will ...

GO DEEPER!
Please refer to **Day 54** in the workbook.

NOTES

Day 55: God and Jesus Have You

"In the beginning God created the heaven and the earth."

—Genesis 1:1 KJV

"The grace of our Lord Jesus Christ be with you all. Amen."

—Revelations 22:21 KJV

From beginning to end God has us in His hands. What was the first thing that came to your mind when you woke up this morning? When my eyes open, for me it is simple— "Thank you" is my first thought; thanking God for another day. Sometimes it may be, "Is it true? Am I dreaming?" as I'm so grateful for this blessing. Jesus wants us to help build God's Kingdom here on Earth. He wants us to build and protect his church. Not just the physical structure, but the spiritual one found only through him. The last words published in the Bible are so inspiring, encouraging, and uplifting.

Jesus' grace will be with all of us, not some of us, but all of us. Up every mountain, down every valley, through every forest and desert, in the sky and in the water, and even low below the deepest depths of the earth. Jesus and God are with us. We can leave our planet, this galaxy, and guess what? Nothing changes as far as Jesus and our Father are concerned. Is that not amazing? They show up and show out every day for us. What would life be like if we showed up and showed out representing them to the fullest? The world truly would be a better place! Why not do our part and start today! Nope, I didn't say tomorrow—I said TODAY! Enjoy the rest of your day. Breathe in that beautiful smell of life and love, provided by our heavenly Father.

PRAYER

Father, everything You have done has had a specific purpose and plan. Everything is done at a specific time, designated only by You. You laid the foundation, made us to respectfully have dominion over all other creatures, and You presented us with Your laws. We repeatedly and consistently disobey those laws, mismanage the land, animals, and resources. You sent Your son, Jesus, to show us the way, but we were too blinded by our fears and lusts to follow him.

You sent us the Holy Spirit/Ghost, and that reality was too deep of water for us to want to dive into. From the very first to the very last sentence in the Bible, You have given us the tools to use and the examples to learn from. I want to see, Lord. I want to learn. I want to be the best example I can be as a steward in Your Kingdom. Father open me up so that I can see inside. I thank You now for this blessing. In Your Son Jesus' name, I pray. Amen.

SPEAK YOUR TRUTH

Say the words below and write beside them your truth. You can also use the workbook to write your responses.

- I Feel…
- I Am…
- I Believe…
- I Am Grateful For…
- I Will Improve…
- I Am Proud of Myself Because…
- I Will Stay Out of My/God's Way By…

Today I Will Focus More on...
And Focus Less on...
Today I Will ...

GO DEEPER!
Please refer to **Day 55** in the workbook.

NOTES

Day 56: Wait For Your Harvest

Another parable He put forth to them, saying: "The kingdom of heaven is like a man who sowed good seed in his field; but while men slept, his enemy came and sowed tares among the wheat and went his way. But when the grain had sprouted and produced a crop, then the tares also appeared.

—Matthew 13:24-26 NKJV

We all have enemies, clear and present, and some that are silently waiting in the darkness. You can't control what they say or do to you and your crops. You can't keep them from planting tares next to your wheat. You can't keep them from spreading lies about you. What you can do is wait for the harvest. Wait for your wheat to grow healthy and strong. Then you swiftly and effectively snatch those tares and burn them to nothingness. Exactly what the "liar" is— NOTHING!

You need to let God's truth and light shine over your enemy's lies and darkness. Don't hastily try to fight this battle alone. Don't jump and snatch up the tares before harvest, and risk killing off your valuable wheat! Don't rush to dispel lies against you. Let the truth be revealed and let that proof squash your enemy like a disease-ridden bug! At the same time, don't look at the tares and give up on your wheat. Don't start thinking that they won't grow healthy, then decide to sow seed elsewhere. Continue to water, fertilize, protect, and nurture your seeds. So don't waste a moment not being open and honest with the one you love. Don't split your time between two or more fields. Focus your time and attention on that one field, building that one relationship. Don't let your focus be on what someone else is planting. That can make what you have look less desirable. What that other person brings might be tares, they may be your enemy and not your friend. Tend to the field in your relationship, and watch the fruits of your labor come harvest!

PRAYER

Father, thank You for blessing me with another day. One more day You have allowed me to be a blessing to someone else. One more day You have allowed me to prove my devotion to You and Your Kingdom. As I plant my good seeds, water them, and nurture them, I cannot keep my eyes on my crops every second of the day. I cannot protect myself and my crop from someone motivated by the "liar", who seeks to destroy the work that I have done in Your name.

Father, I pray for Your protection. I pray that the tares don't squeeze the life out of my wheat. That the sight of those ugly weeds doesn't cause me or someone else to uproot the entire crop prematurely. Or abandon them and sow seed elsewhere. Help me to see as in this parable, that once harvested, I can gather the tares in bundles and burn them. Then take my wheat to store in my barn. With You Lord, I can save my crops. Show me the way. Teach me how to be patient, and to see through the weeds my enemy has planted, straight to my crops of sustenance. Amen.

SPEAK YOUR TRUTH

Say the words below and write beside them your truth. You can also use the workbook to write your responses.

> I Feel...
> I Am...
> I Believe...
> I Am Grateful For...

I Will Improve...
I Am Proud of Myself Because...
I Will Stay Out of My/God's Way By...
Today I Will Focus More on...
And Focus Less on...
Today I Will...

GO DEEPER!
Please refer to **Day 56** in the workbook.

NOTES

Day 57: Be On Your Guard

Be on your guard; stand firm in the faith; be courageous; be strong. Do everything in love.

—1 Corinthians 16:13-14 NIV

God's love is amazing. We love because He first loved us. In the storm we must be brave, we must know that it will pass and that God is there every millisecond. We must be comforted in this knowledge and comfortable enough to sleep on that rocky boat. Just as Jesus did while his disciples freaked out watching the crashing waves and lightning strikes. Jesus never did anything out of fear, bitterness, resentment, or hate. Jesus did and said everything in love. Even when he disagreed with someone, he did so with love—knowing that God's truth was all he needed. Jesus knew that God was always right—that He is the answer to all questions—He is the resolution to all conflict. He is the compass when we are lost. He is the anchor when our boat needs to be secured and stable.

We must do everything in love. When we know it is time to end a relationship, we must do it in love. Lovingly end it and walk away. There is never a need for closure when you leave in love. I don't need closure for any relationship I have ever been in. Because I know that I loved those individuals and that I still love them as Jesus instructed. Not romantically but in Christ. Relationships that I know were not of God,

I can confidently say I ended in love. Without hesitation and without doubt or regret. I am now filled with so much wisdom, I can easily discern those individuals that are mere tests of my moral fiber. The tests of the forbidden fruit that are in front of me to see whether I will bite the fruit or lovingly walk away. The visual and emotional appeal that tugs at our gut are not messages and urges of our heavenly Father. That's the enemy—the "liar" toying with us.

It is our fear of being perceived as mean, cold, and callous that keeps us connected with someone we're not supposed to be with. It is our desire to fill a void that keeps us from walking away. Or never entering the relationship, to begin with. It is us once again trying to think like God, be like God, and do His work. In our desire to feel complete we use another person, instead of God. That is what causes us to spend our valuable time with someone He has no intention of you being with.

God gives us the freedom to choose the flesh and the world, or Him. He's patient. He believes in us when we don't. He waits while we detour on a perceived shortcut that turns out to be the long way and the wrong way. We must follow God's instructions. We must walk in faith and know that He never directs our paths to places where He is not. It is only when we stray do we find heartache, confusion, pain, and drama. It is then we must learn our lesson for as long as it takes to learn it! Why can't we follow Him and lead a life of love, peace, tranquility, and joy? Have an amazing day. Be on your guard. Stand firm in the faith. Be courageous and strong—and remember to do everything in love! God bless you.

PRAYER

Father, keep me alert and focused on You. I have a lot of bumps and bruises that I acquired over the years, I've even had my share this year. I've been disappointed and hurt by people I love. Your Word says to do everything in love. So I know this to mean that even when deceived and neglected, my responses and reactions are to be in and from love. Father, fill me with the courage and strength to endure all. Give me the vision to see what is around me and before me. When something negative comes my way, hold me, Father. That I might breathe and let You handle the situation. I want to be courageous Father. I want to be able to withstand the storm. I want to be able to look in the eyes of those who would and have caused me harm, and all that they see in my eyes is Your love. All honor and praises go to You Lord. In Your name, I humbly pray. Amen.

SPEAK YOUR TRUTH

Say the words below and write beside them your truth. You can also use the workbook to write your responses.

> I Feel…
> I Am…
> I Believe…
> I Am Grateful For…
> I Will Improve…
> I Am Proud of Myself Because…
> I Will Stay Out of My/God's Way By…
> Today I Will Focus More on…
> And Focus Less on…
> Today I Will …

GO DEEPER!

Please refer to **Day 57** in the workbook.

NOTES

Day 58: What You Give, You Get

Behold, I will make you small among the nations; you shall be utterly despised. The pride of your heart has deceived you, you who live in the clefts of the rock, in your lofty dwelling, who say in your heart, Who will bring me down to the ground? Though you soar aloft like the eagle, though your nest is set among the stars, from there I will bring you down, declares the Lord.

—Obadiah 1:2-4 KJV

Never get too full of yourself. Never get comfortable enough to say, "*I did this*", when the truth is, God is your source. He is your knowledge and wisdom, and the reason you have your many gifts and talents. Your declaration should always be that all that you have is because of God's will and grace. We all need a reminder that it's not all about us. It's about God and our service to and for Him. Your material riches are God-given, and just as He gives He can take away. So be sure to give freely of your time, money, and other resources to those that lack what you have. Don't be so quick to say, "*I did it, so they need to go out and get theirs on their own as I did!*" Or as the saying goes, "*I got mine. Now go get yours!*"

God has many ways to snatch you from your high-placed nest, and put you at the same level or below the very people you looked down upon. Remember that you get what you give! Enjoy your day. Give it your all, focusing more on doing an excellent job than staring at the clock waiting to leave. There are millions of people without jobs, thousands would gladly take your position. So work like you are honored to have it! I don't care if you have given notice or were given notice, let your last moments be some of your best!

PRAYER

Father free me from being prideful, greedy, envious, spiteful, arrogant, vain, superficial. And a lover of money, power, and material possessions. Keep me, humble Lord. I know that what I have in this world is by Your doing and Your blessings. When I forget my place and refuse to walk righteously, it is Your will that grounds me and snatches me back down to the place of humbleness. Thank You, Father. Amen.

SPEAK YOUR TRUTH

Say the words below and write beside them your truth. You can also use the workbook to write your responses.

> I Feel…
> I Am…
> I Believe…
> I Am Grateful For…
> I Will Improve…
> I Am Proud of Myself Because…
> I Will Stay Out of My/God's Way By…
> Today I Will Focus More on…
> And Focus Less on…
> Today I Will …

GO DEEPER!

Please refer to **Day 58** in the workbook.

NOTES

Day 59: Faith

And without faith, it's impossible to please God, because anyone that comes to him must believe he exists and that he rewards those who earnestly seek him.

—Hebrews 11:6 NIV

Women, if your husband didn't believe in you and doubted your love and loyalty how would you feel? Men, how would you feel if your wife questioned your ability to provide for your family? Now magnify that by the zillionth power and that's how God feels when we have little or no faith in Him. Even if you only have faith as small as a mustard seed, it will change your life. Some of us don't even push the limits that far. When you can't believe in yourself or others—that you can see and touch daily—believe in Him, He's never steered you wrong. He makes the impossible possible. We just don't believe it until we see it, and that is why we don't see and experience more.

PRAYER
Father, thank You for giving me another day to serve and worship You. Thank You for Your patience. As I sometimes waver from total faith to half faith. To a faith that lies somewhere between a mustard seed and grain of rice. Thank You for loving me anyway. Thank You for the trials in my life that ultimately helped and help me to develop my character. Thank You for allowing me to see

that struggle does not always equate to something that I did wrong. But rather, what is required of me to endure what yet is to come. The struggle also encourages me to turn to You more and turn less inwardly. Where I always get myself into trouble. I'm so glad that I know You, and that You live in and through me.

I'm glad that I have this relationship with You and I want to strengthen and deepen it. So that I am in better alignment with You. I want to walk by faith, not by sight. I want to walk by faith, not by fear and desperation. I want to walk by faith, not reacting to my circumstances. I want to stand firmly in my knowledge that there is no power or presence greater than You. There is no understanding greater than Yours. Help me to surrender fully to You so that I might be free. Help me to walk, speak, think, and be as You desire. I pray to please You, Lord. Amen.

SPEAK YOUR TRUTH

Say the words below and write beside them your truth. You can also use the workbook to write your responses.

I Feel...
I Am...
I Believe...
I Am Grateful For...
I Will Improve...
I Am Proud of Myself Because...
I Will Stay Out of My/God's Way By...
Today I Will Focus More on...
And Focus Less on...
Today I Will ...

GO DEEPER!

Please refer to **Day 59** in the workbook.

NOTES

Day 60: Letting Go Of Your Past

...but this one thing I do, forgetting those things which are behind, and reaching toward what is ahead.

—Philippians 3:13 KJV

Don't confuse "forgetting our past" with a history that we must remember to never repeat. Slavery, genocide, etc. should never be forgotten. I'm not one to look for past loves. But if you do, this word is for you. Let them go. Move forward. Ask God to free you from looking for what once was but no longer. Old images of a past that brought you more pain than joy, you need to let go. Forgive them and yourself then walk away. God makes no mistakes. Don't carry around baggage not meant for you!

PRAYER

Father, I choose to forget the pain of the past, in the ways that I hold on and refuse to move forward. Holding on to my darkened thoughts means that I doubt Your ability to rectify what happened. It means that I'm stuck in a time that I refuse to leave, even though You're calling on and waiting for me to leave. I want to let go of what once was so that I can embrace what is still yet to be. I'm missing out on so much of today, of the present, because my mind is in the past. I don't want anything to hold me back from the future that You have prepared for me. I choose forgiveness and ask that You help me press forward in every area of my life. Free me from the thinking of woulda, shoulda, coulda. So that I may be at peace with life as it is now. Then I may reach my hand into the future of tomorrow. Amen.

SPEAK YOUR TRUTH

Say the words below and write beside them your truth. You can also use the workbook to write your responses.

> I Feel...
> I Am...
> I Believe...
> I Am Grateful For...
> I Will Improve...
> I Am Proud of Myself Because...
> I Will Stay Out of My/God's Way By...
> Today I Will Focus More on...
> And Focus Less on...
> Today I Will ...

GO DEEPER!

Please refer to **Day 60** in the workbook.

NOTES

Day 61: God Hears Us, Even In Our Silence

But some said, "This man healed a blind man. Couldn't he have kept Lazarus from dying?" Jesus was still angry as he arrived at the tomb, a cave with a stone rolled across its entrance. "Roll the stone aside," Jesus told them. But Martha, the dead man's sister, protested, "Lord, he has been dead for four days. The smell will be terrible." Jesus responded, "Didn't I tell you that you would see God's glory if you believe?" So they rolled the stone aside. Then Jesus looked up to heaven and said, "Father, thank you for hearing me. You always hear me, but I said it out loud for the sake of all these people standing here, so that they will believe you sent me." Then Jesus shouted, "Lazarus, come out!" And the dead man came out, his hands and feet bound in graveclothes, his face wrapped in a headcloth. Jesus told them, "Unwrap him and let him go!"

—John 11:37-44 NLT

Our prayers we speak aloud are not for God to hear. We speak aloud for us to hear, comprehend, and reflect on what we are saying, asking, and declaring to God and Jesus. We need to hear what we're declaring to ourselves. We also are speaking to the mortal mind that can easily be manipulated into serving the enemy. It is in direct opposition to our heavenly Father. We must remember that we are spiritual beings, reflections of God, here in human form. Once our time here is up we resume our lives eternally in spiritual form. Jesus proved more than once that our bodies are shells and that death is unreal. By resurrecting those that were perceived to be deceased in every sense of the term— he showed the power of God. He showed that our reality in the world is not God's reality. He taught that if we want to reach a higher level of understanding, to get closer to God, and to be more like him we have to believe without a shadow of doubt in God.

We have to believe that God is omniscient, omnipresent, and omnipotent supreme. We can not merely say it and brag about it when comparing gods. We must know deep in the recesses of our minds and souls that God is who we claim Him to be. And that He has the will and power to do all the things we have read about and preach every week. We have to believe in Him more than we believe the birth certificate that confirms our birth parents. And that the red stoplight means stop, and that fire burns and consumes material things. We have to believe that when that voice in our mind speaks to us and warns us of harm it is that of God's. We have to believe that the voice that says, "*Turn right not left*" and steers us the correct direction, is God's voice speaking to us. That the voice that says, "*Everything is taken care of My child*" is God's voice. We must BELIEVE!

PRAYER

Father thank You for always hearing me. Thank You for taking care of my needs. Faith means believing without seeing, hearing, or touching. To believe in You and Your son means to receive endless blessings and eternal life beyond our human form. Father I don't have to pray aloud for You to hear me. I don't need to have a conversation with You aloud for You to answer my questions, and handle my problems. You always hear me, Lord. Thank You. Jesus said that all we have to do is believe, and each day my faith in You and him grows stronger. Each day I release more of my cares, concerns, fears, hopes, aspira-

tions, dreams, and goals to You Father. Thank You for Your love and patience Lord. Thank You for Your grace. Amen.

SPEAK YOUR TRUTH

Say the words below and write beside them your truth. You can also use the workbook to write your responses.

> I Feel...
> I Am...
> I Believe...
> I Am Grateful For...
> I Will Improve...
> I Am Proud of Myself Because...
> I Will Stay Out of My/God's Way By...
> Today I Will Focus More on...
> And Focus Less on...
> Today I Will ...

GO DEEPER!

Please refer to **Day 61** in the workbook.

NOTES

Day 62: Being Prepared For Your Blessings

Give us this day our daily bread.

—Matthew 6:11 KJV

Every day God provides for you. Both little and big, obvious and not so obvious. Be sure that when you do ask for blessings that you have your baskets ready to be filled with God's bread!

PRAYER
Father, thank You for Your grace and favor on my life today. I know You have a fresh supply of everything that I need. I know that You can fill my physical, spiritual, emotional, and financial needs. Help me trust You more as I seek Your guiding light. I'm praying for more faith because I know that it displeases You when I don't simply believe in You. Give me strength Father. Amen.

SPEAK YOUR TRUTH
Say the words below and write beside them your truth. You can also use the workbook to write your responses.

I Feel...

I Am...
I Believe...
I Am Grateful For...
I Will Improve...
I Am Proud of Myself Because...
I Will Stay Out of My/God's Way By...
Today I Will Focus More on...
And Focus Less on...
Today I Will ...

GO DEEPER!
Please refer to **Day 62** in the workbook.

NOTES

GO BEYOND: Month 2

DEEPER STUDY

This section is devoted to deeper study, reflection, and analysis as you end the month and begin your focus on next month. You may not be ready for this step at this moment. Please know that if you ever feel overwhelmed, you can return to this activity at a later date.

If you want, feel free to record today's session using video or audio. It can help you with further prayer and reflection.

1. Look at your notes from Days 23 and 24. Can you recall those days? Can you recall how you felt, the things that you heard, and said?
2. How have you been progressing with your conversations with God? Has it become easier to speak freely to God?
3. Close your eyes and breathe slowly.
   Inhale through your nose and exhale through your mouth. Continue breathing slowly until your thoughts also slow down. It may take a few minutes. Allow the process to unfold, don't rush it. You can sit or lie down. Just make sure that you're in a relaxed position and state of mind.
4. Slowly say these words aloud, "God show me what You see for me". Keep repeating this until a picture begins to form in your mind. It may take longer for you if your mind has a lot of clut-

ter or if you haven't practiced having conversations with God. It's okay. There is no right way, just your way. He's not judging how you speak with Him. He just wants to speak with you and broaden your relationship.

5. Ask God, "What does this mean Father?"
Continue asking this question, patiently, making sure to listen and look. Things may not make sense right now. It's okay, just keep inquiring. Ask God the same question in different ways if you need to.
6. Once you reach a point where the conversation is interrupted, thank God for the chat.

Then remain where you are seated (or lying) and reflect over the experience. You may feel emotional, possibly overwhelmed, or just at peace. Let yourself feel what you feel.

Don't try to block or filter what you feel. This is about you connecting with yourself and connecting with God. We're breaking through barriers, we're changing our habits and thinking, and we're pushing to a new level. Take notes, if you can (either during or after this session). You will review these notes again later.

NOTES

MONTH THREE

What Do You See?

So she named Adonai who had spoken with her El Ro'i [God of seeing], because she said, "Have I really seen the One who sees me [and stayed alive]?"

— B'RESHEET 16:13 CJB

[GENESIS 16:13]

Are you ready to see?

PONDER THIS: Month 3

Jesus said during his Sermon on the Mount, "*You have heard that it was said, 'AN EYE FOR AN EYE, AND A TOOTH FOR A TOOTH.' But I say to you, do not resist an evil person; but whoever slaps you on your right cheek, turn the other to him also. If anyone wants to sue you and take your shirt, let him have your coat also. Whoever forces you to go one mile, go with him two.*"[5]

What are your thoughts about this? What is the first thing that comes to your mind? Write your thoughts and opinions below. Visit the **Consider This: Month 3** section towards the back of the book. There I share insight into these verses and possibly challenge your views about what they truly mean. Maybe you will learn something new that you can share with others.

Day 63: Know Your Truth...You're Already Equipped

He was preaching: "Someone more powerful than I will come after me. I am not worthy to stoop down and untie the strap of His sandals. I have baptized you with water, but He will baptize you with the Holy Spirit."

—Mark 1:7-8 HCSB

God equipped John the Baptist with the resources to prepare the people for the coming of Jesus. Some believed, prepared, and waited—most did not. Just like the vast majority did not realize who John the Baptist truly was and his purpose. How many people are we ignoring, overlooking, doubting, or too busy or frustrated to wait for? How many experiences have been missed blessings?

On the flip side, how many people were you supposed to avoid but you invested time and energy in them? How many situations did you enter that you were supposed to bypass? How many paths did you walk down that wasn't intended for you? We must open our eyes, ears, hearts, and minds to God so that we are never disconnected from even a faint whisper from Him. You may expect to see huge glaring signs. When the smallest of them—that you overlook—actually speak louder. Don't over-analyze or rationalize, just be open to receive the answer.

PRAYER

Father, You prepare us for what's yet to come. It must be disappointing when we don't listen, believe, and prepare to receive. You send people, show signs, and deliver messages. I want to be ready and willing to experience all that You have to offer. I want to be receptive to everything You send my way. I pray for discernment and patience. I pray for insight. I want to be all that You want me to be. I want to fully embrace every person and experience intended for me that You send down my path. In Jesus' name, I pray. Amen.

SPEAK YOUR TRUTH

Say the words below and write beside them your truth. You can also use the workbook to write your responses.

I Feel…
I Am…
I Believe…
I Am Grateful For…
I Will Improve…
I Am Proud of Myself Because…
I Will Stay Out of My/God's Way By…
Today I Will Focus More on…
And Focus Less on…
Today I Will …

GO DEEPER!

Please refer to **Day 63** in the workbook.

NOTES

Day 64: God's Gift is Within You

Therefore I remind you to stir up the gift of God which is in you... For God has not given us the spirit of fear, but of power and of love and of a sound mind.

—2 Timothy 1:6-7 NKJV

We are fully equipped with everything we need. God has provided an endless supply of tools and gifts to be used to build His Kingdom. To spread His love and grace. To restore dignity, hope, and honor to those who are struggling most. And to put (and keep) in check those who have strayed, and believe these gifts to be theirs to do whatever they please. Even if that means harming others in the process. Let us not walk in fear, because that is not a quality or gift of God. Let us remember our roles as His servants, stewards—His children; that we always honor and obey Him. Use the gifts that you were born with to heal, help, and uplift God's children. Starting today!

PRAYER

Father thank You for Your priceless gifts. I will use the power, love, and mind You have given me to do good in Your name. I will do so without fear, arro-

gance, or a sense of entitlement or superiority. I honor and love You all the days of my life. Amen.

SPEAK YOUR TRUTH

Say the words below and write beside them your truth. You can also use the workbook to write your responses.

> I Feel...
> I Am...
> I Believe...
> I Am Grateful For...
> I Will Improve...
> I Am Proud of Myself Because...
> I Will Stay Out of My/God's Way By...
> Today I Will Focus More on...
> And Focus Less on...
> Today I Will ...

GO DEEPER!

Please refer to **Day 64** in the workbook.

NOTES

Day 65: Your Life Reflects Your Relationship With God

Know ye not that ye are the temple of God, and that the Spirit of God dwelleth in you?

Let no man deceive himself. If any man among you seemeth to be wise in this world, let him become a fool, that he may be wise. For the wisdom of this world is foolishness with God. For it is written, He taketh the wise in their own craftiness. And again, The Lord knoweth the thoughts of the wise, that they are vain.

Therefore let no man glory in men. For all things are yours; Whether Paul, or Apollos, or Cephas, or the world, or life, or death, or things present, or things to come; all are yours; And ye are Christ's; and Christ is God's.

—I Corinthians 3:16,18-23 KJV

Be focused on knowing, expressing, and living God's Word and His plan for you, not that of the world. God isn't concerned with what facts you can recall about worldly things. He wants to know and see what you are doing with the knowledge He is empowering You with to build His Kingdom. He could care less about the latest gossip, fashion, or lyrics to a song you heard on the radio. He is concerned with what is in you, and what you are doing to combat the temptations in and of the world. What legacy are you leaving behind when you are no longer living on this level of existence? You are His ambassador always reflecting Him every single day. How we think, what we say, and how we live our lives is a direct reflection of our relationship with God. And what we are portraying as His child and representative. Protect your mind and body from pollutants that slowly eat away at you. Then like a plague, creeps into the lives of your brothers and sisters. Feed others, don't poison them!

Don't find comfort in "*My pastor said*" when you can have surety in "*Jesus said*" and "*God said*". Don't be overly confident in your wisdom, or claiming it as your own. For true wisdom comes only from one place, and that is God. Don't let Him have to put you in your place! Make sure that every place you go, and every person that you interact with, that you are reflecting God's love. As an ambassador of excellence should! Be blessed and be a blessing to others.

PRAYER

Father thank You. Thank You for teaching, guiding, nurturing, correcting, and molding me. Father I don't want to be of the world, I want to be a tool for the world. To make it a better, more wholesome, and righteous place. I want to be fluent in Your Word. Not the world's vices and trappings through the media. Not the word of religious zealots focused on pushing their agenda and not Yours. If it's not focused on helping Your children become better stewards and ambassadors for You, then I don't want to have anything to do with it.

Father when I appear to be straying from Your path, turning from Your ways, please steer me back straight. When my mind thinks thoughts that go against Your teachings, realign me. When the words that flow from my mouth are anything but Christ-like, apply loving pressure to my clay. Help me to see Your ways. Correct my thinking and speech to resemble that of Your son, Jesus. The truest model of Your spiritual reflection. Let my daily walk not be too easy

Lord, because no great masterpiece was ever created quickly and with ease. There were always moments of friction, revisions, delays, and missteps. I want a lifetime of learned lessons. I shouldn't master life anytime soon, no matter if I'm 40, 60, 80, or a ripe youthful age of 100.

You should always be a mystery, but I know that I can always come directly to You for answers. Never will I put a human in Your place of authority, dominion, reliance, or parenthood. You forever will be my eternal Father-Mother God, all-harmonious. In Your son, Jesus' name I humbly pray and give thanks this day. Amen.

SPEAK YOUR TRUTH
Say the words below and write beside them your truth. You can also use the workbook to write your responses.

> I Feel...
> I Am...
> I Believe...
> I Am Grateful For...
> I Will Improve...
> I Am Proud of Myself Because...
> I Will Stay Out of My/God's Way By...
> Today I Will Focus More on...
> And Focus Less on...
> Today I Will ...

GO DEEPER!
Please refer to **Day 65** in the workbook.

NOTES

Day 66: How Deep and Great is Your Love?

I thank my God, making mention of you always in my prayers, hearing of your love and faith which you have toward the Lord Jesus and toward all the saints, that the sharing of your faith may become effective by the acknowledgment of every good thing which is in you in Christ Jesus. For we have great joy and consolation in your love, because the hearts of the saints have been refreshed by you, brother.

—Philemon 1:4-7 NKJV

Philemon speaks of his love and faith in the passages referenced above. How deep and how great is your love for God and His Son, Jesus Christ? How faithful are you to them, to God's plan and His purpose for you? How faithful are you in your walk to be more like Jesus?

We all stumble, falter, and forget our promise to be Christ-like. I too must watch what I'm thinking and the words that I speak. I can say something that I know I wouldn't say in church, in front of many of my elders, or in mixed company. So why would I allow myself to speak and think such negative things that are the polar opposite of Christ? Every day we must fight the "liar" who says, *"It's okay this time"*. As soon as things go wrong, the liar says, *"Uh oh you're gonna get it now, God isn't go-*

ing to forgive you for that... this one is a biggie!" We must tune out the "liar" and every time something negative comes to mind we must stop and say, "*Shut up. You're a liar!*" Then thank God for protecting your thoughts and deterring you from speaking or behaving negatively.

For what we think and speak about we bring about, it is the natural flow of life. Let's focus on being positive and being a blessing to others.

PRAYER
Thank You, Father! What more could be said to express my appreciation for all that You have, are, and will do for me? Thank You for providing gifts such as the Bible and the exemplar—Your Son, Jesus. Thank You for the leaders anointed by You since the beginning of time, whose stories are told in Your holy book. Thank You for Your protecting angels. They whisper in my ear words of caution as well as enlightenment and encouragement. You delivered these blessings to me Father. You deliver blessings to me in physical, metaphysical, and spiritual forms. No man could do this. Man can't provide constant and unconditional care, love, guidance, and support like You. Thank You, Father. Amen.

SPEAK YOUR TRUTH
Say the words below and write beside them your truth. You can also use the workbook to write your responses.

I Feel...
I Am...
I Believe...
I Am Grateful For...
I Will Improve...
I Am Proud of Myself Because...
I Will Stay Out of My/God's Way By...
Today I Will Focus More on...
And Focus Less on...
Today I Will ...

GO DEEPER!
Please refer to **Day 66** in the workbook.

NOTES

Day 67: What Have You Been Called to Do?

"If you refuse to take up your cross and follow me, you are not worthy of being mine."

—Matthew 10:38 NLT

If life were easy, didn't require lessons to be learned, and sacrifices to be made—then Jesus never would have had to take up the cross. He wouldn't have needed to show that God is all-in-all, and can heal all, save all, and provide strength to all. He would have never endured the physical and mental torture. We all must go through the valleys and face those mountainsides. We must believe and know that God can level those valleys and mountains to flat land for us to walk on. Realizing that it is only in our walk with Jesus that makes that possible. It is only through the demonstration that our belief is strengthened. We must not merely talk the talk, we must walk the walk. We must carry that heavy cross, pray through the attacks and ridicule, and know that God is there with us and for us.

    I don't share posts on **BreakingBreadWithNatasha.com** because my life is blissful and easy breezy. It's not free of pain, debt, heartaches, and disappointments. No, I share it because just like many of you I go through the ups and downs of life. I get beat down and have to find the strength to get back up. Some days I don't want to get out of bed or leave the house. I have experienced so much loss and pain that there are moments when I wonder if I can take anymore. But somehow I endure. I must. There's no option B. I know that I am here for a purpose. Until I fulfill that purpose I will stay prayed up and ready to take on the battles every single day.

I post messages on my blog because God touched my heart to do so. He showed me that even in my moments of agony I can always find a way to serve Him. I can always find a way to make someone feel and know that whatever they are going through—it WILL be alright. For every smile I help bring to the face of someone in pain, it helps me manage what I am going through. So understand that I am not sharing these things because I believe that I'm at a certain level or above anyone else.

I am everyone else. God has merely found another way to work through me. A way I never would have fathomed. But I am grateful because it has brought me closer to Him. It has made me a better student. It has made me more loving, caring, patient, considerate, and understanding. I also know that by spreading God's Word I can't one day just say, "*Okay life is better for me now. No sense in sending these messages to folks*". I know it doesn't work that way. I know that my life will never be free of hang-ups, slip-ups, and running into concrete walls.

My life is a constant demonstration. Maybe I have been called by God to serve in this capacity. Maybe something beyond this—I don't know and I won't question Him. I will merely get up every day, read the Word, pray, and let Him guide me to the passage that needs to be heard for that day. As I pray to Him I will type, then send my messages to my subscribers. As I type these words I can't help but smile. Because never in my wildest dreams did I think I would have a blog that focused on expressing and sharing God's love through a spiritual lens. Never did I imagine writing a book inspired by that blog. God is awesome!

I love each and every one of you, even if I have never met you—I love you. I pray for you and I hope you are praying for me. Together in prayer, we can all see our ways through—because God never lets our prayers go unanswered.

PRAYER

Father, today I am on my knees humbled. My faith has not wavered although the pressures of the world are closing in on me. Please give me strength Lord. I have obligations that I have not kept, and my honor is being questioned, Father. What do we do when we have fallen on to hard times but so many other people have also fallen on hard times? I pray to You for guidance. I'm putting aside my pride, postponing plans, deferring instant gratification, and forgiving others. Just as I have never intended to hurt people, I have to believe that others have not intended to hurt me. I won't let this situation beat me down.

I will not let this situation sway my attention from serving You and Your children. I will follow Jesus. And know that everything that I am going through is making me a better, stronger, wiser, and more disciplined servant. I don't want my tears of pain to ever make You and Jesus think that I don't believe, that I am giving in and giving up. Father I know You will never forsake me. I know that You will never leave me. I know that You are here with me always—watching, protecting, and taking care of me. I hope that I'm not taking these facts for granted. I never want to be casual about my relationship with You. I know that it is up to me to find ways to adapt to my circumstances. I know that Jesus has already cleared my path—but it is my cross to bear. I must take those steps. I'm walking, Father. In Jesus' name, I humbly pray to You. Amen.

SPEAK YOUR TRUTH

Say the words below and write beside them your truth. You can also use the workbook to write your responses.

> I Feel...
> I Am...
> I Believe...
> I Am Grateful For...
> I Will Improve...
> I Am Proud of Myself Because...
> I Will Stay Out of My/God's Way By...
> Today I Will Focus More on...

And Focus Less on...
Today I Will ...

GO DEEPER!
Please refer to **Day 67** in the workbook.

NOTES

Day 68: The Seed and The Sower

"Listen! Consider the sower who went out to sow. As he sowed, this occurred: Some seed fell along the path, and the birds came and ate it up. Other seed fell on rocky ground where it didn't have much soil, and it sprang up right away, since it didn't have deep soil. When the sun came up, it was scorched, and since it didn't have a root, it withered. Other seed fell among thorns, and the thorns came up and choked it, and it didn't produce a crop. Still others fell on good ground and produced a crop that increased 30, 60, and 100 times [what was sown]."

—Mark 4:3-8 HCSB

There are billions of humans roaming this planet each day. For this reflection, we won't try to consider the humans on distant planets we've never seen. I mean, seriously, why would we think that God would limit Himself to creating life solely on this planet? That would be foolish of us. But rather than going down that mental rabbit hole, let's just think about the human life on Earth. We are God's seeds. We are also sowers of seeds. There are some seeds that fall along the wayside and are consumed by spiritual vultures. There are some seeds that are in unstable and chaotic environments. Their ecosystems don't provide for the seeds to grow at the right time and with deep roots. Their impatience or lack of resources causes them to rush the process, face devastating failure, and give up.

There are seeds that happen to be in environments and in relationships that always leave them under attack. There is no reprieve, no time-out, and no grace period. It is combative from the beginning to the end. They are always in a constant state of warfare. They never have the time and energy to produce anything of quality. These seeds are consumers because their efforts never produce anything of benefit. Then, there are the seeds that have a great foundation. They have healthy soil in which to grow deep and strong roots. They have the right environment that allows for the production of upwards of 100 times what was sown. Which seed are you? Do you know? Can you tell? How can you tell? Think about it and then share your thoughts in the notes section.

Looking through the lens of the sower of seeds, there are some things to pay close attention to. Seeds can be thoughts, the words that we speak, and the way that we treat others. Seeds can be the actions that we take, how we invest our time and money, and how we produce other human offspring. With those perspectives, consider this—where are you casting your seeds? Where and how are they being sown? Are you being intentional, casual, or reckless with the sowing process? Are you mindful of how your crop may impact others? Is your crop a positive or negative representation of you and your relationship with God?

PRAYER

Father, I pray for peace and light within my life, and the lives of those that I know and don't know. I pray for my soul to be kept right with You. I pray for good health and the wisdom to make the right decisions as You see fit. I pray that I am a good seed with a healthy foundation that benefits Your Kingdom greatly.

SPEAK YOUR TRUTH

Say the words below and write beside them your truth. You can also use the workbook to write your responses.

I Feel...
I Am...
I Believe...
I Am Grateful For...
I Will Improve...
I Am Proud of Myself Because...
I Will Stay Out of My/God's Way By...
Today I Will Focus More on...
And Focus Less on...
Today I Will ...

GO DEEPER!

Please refer to **Day 68** in the workbook.

NOTES

Day 69: See Deeper

You simple people, use good judgment. You foolish people, show some understanding. My words are plain to anyone with understanding, clear to those with knowledge. Choose my instruction rather than silver, and knowledge rather than pure gold. For wisdom is far more valuable than rubies. Nothing you desire can compare with it. I, Wisdom, live together with good judgment. I know where to discover knowledge and discernment. Common sense and success belong to me. Insight and strength are mine. The Lord formed me from the beginning, before he created anything else.

—Proverbs 8:5, 9-12, 14, 22 NLT

Pray to God for the wisdom to learn from past errors and to make sound decisions now, and in the future. Pray to Him for the strength and common sense to see things as they are. And act accordingly, as a righteous practitioner of His Truth.

PRAYER

Father open my eyes and ears. Let me see and hear what I'm supposed to know when I'm supposed to know it. Control my tongue and what I say so that I am only speaking words of Your truth and rightness. I pray for wisdom Lord. I pray for good judgment that walks hand-in-hand with wisdom so that I make the right decisions at the right time. Increase my ability to see deeper Lord, let my insight be magnified. In Jesus' name, I humbly pray. Amen.

SPEAK YOUR TRUTH

Say the words below and write beside them your truth. You can also use the workbook to write your responses.

I Feel…
I Am…
I Believe…
I Am Grateful For…
I Will Improve…
I Am Proud of Myself Because…
I Will Stay Out of My/God's Way By…
Today I Will Focus More on…
And Focus Less on…
Today I Will …

GO DEEPER!

Please refer to **Day 69** in the workbook.

NOTES

Day 70: Be True to Your Word

"Simply let your 'Yes' be 'Yes,' and your 'No,' 'No'. Anything more comes from the evil one."

—Matthew 5:37 BSB

Not only is it unfair to not speak what we mean when we mean it, but it also goes against God's Word. If you don't want to do something, don't want to go somewhere, don't want to be in a relationship simply say so. Don't say yes when your heart and wisdom are screaming no. The same is true when you truly want to do something—say so. I struggle with this myself. There are times when I want to say no but instead, I say yes—and vice versa. Now don't get me wrong, sometimes changing answers is healthy and beneficial. For instance, switching from an unhealthy to a healthy lifestyle is a great reason to turn your no to a yes. Or leaving an unhealthy relationship even though you tell yourself, *"But I love him/her"*.

What this scripture is digging at is the annoyance that comes from wishy-washy thinking and behavior; when you straddle the fence and can't seem to make up your mind; when it feels more like double-talk than straight talk. God doesn't do confusion. It's either a yes or a no. God doesn't say, *"Hmmm let me think about it"* or *"Well I was considering this but maybe that other thing would be better*". He doesn't commit to one thing and then, later on, scream, "*I change my mind!*" He makes a decision. He keeps His word. When you raise your hand or cast your ballot in a vote, let it be your strongest convictions that move you to this decision. The world has way too many "oops" decisions that we have and still suffer through. On the other side of this argument—let's be clear, once you make a decision, stand by that decision. Don't start backtracking and moonwalking, when you realize that things aren't going as planned, so now you're looking for the escape route. If you messed up, then own up to that mess.

There are times when we must change our decision, change the direction on our chartered course, and pivot another way. It could be a cause for safety, preservation, or because a better way has made itself known. Maybe we began the journey going the wrong way, but we were determined to continue on that route. Well, that's just silly. But we all do it. We stick to our guns and bury our heads in the sand. Because our ego can't handle the self-imposed embarrassment of discovering that we were wrong. In whole or in part. Once we realize our error and we decide to pivot, then commit wholeheartedly. Don't waver. Don't play a game of hopscotch, especially with circumstances that can have a major impact on you and others. There is a great honor in being the man or woman of your word.

PRAYER

Father thank You for molding me. I pray for the ability to not waver, to not ride the fence in life and love. Father let me not say Yes when I mean No, and vice versa. Remove fear from my heart that would cause me to doubt. Let me stand strong in whatever decisions I make, so that I may live righteously and honorably in Your sight. In Your Son Jesus' name, I pray to you Father. Amen.

SPEAK YOUR TRUTH

Say the words below and write beside them your truth. You can also use the workbook to write your responses.

I Feel...
I Am...
I Believe...
I Am Grateful For...
I Will Improve...
I Am Proud of Myself Because...
I Will Stay Out of My/God's Way By...
Today I Will Focus More on...
And Focus Less on...
Today I Will ...

GO DEEPER!
Please refer to **Day 70** in the workbook.

NOTES

Day 71: Your Plans May Not Be God's Plans

"Wisdom will multiply your days and add years to your life."

—Proverbs 9:11 NLT

We must look for the lesson in each day. What happened to us this morning that opened our eyes to a new reality, a new way, a new understanding? Will you continue to explore a darkened path that you know will lead you to unrighteousness? Or will you turn around and seek God's lighted way? Every time you fall down and pick yourself up, do you think of what got you to that place? And what not to do to avoid the same pitfall in the future? If so, you have learned a lesson and gained wisdom in the process. Only a fool sees a pit in the earth and keeps walking across it when it is clear that they should walk around it. Wisdom teaches you this.

When you see that a situation won't go your way, understand that it's not your way you should be concerned with. It's God's way that is our highest priority. Maybe things aren't going your way, as planned, as expected—because God never intended for you to keep walking down that path. It wasn't His plan and His expectation. Maybe He's waiting for you to gain the wisdom to see the signs, learn the lessons, and move on to the path waiting on you. We're the ones who always want to see things through to the end. God's got bigger plans for us than we could ever imagine. Maybe while we're on Hopeless Road, He's waiting for us to get over to Faith Drive. Which requires us to travel down Surrender Boulevard and Believe Highway. Learn your lessons, gain wisdom, and move on to the next step in your beautifully blessed life.

PRAYER

Father thank You for the lessons, trials, tests, and experiences. Thank You for not making my life easy and without a struggle. I know that everything I've gone through and will go through is to help me grow through learned lessons and wisdom gained. Father I don't want to just be smart, I want wisdom. I want to know some things through other people's experiences. I want to know some things through my own experience. Because I have walked the path, crossed the bridge, and climbed the mountainside. And I may even have the bumps, bruises, and scars to prove it.

My age has nothing to do with how much wisdom I have. Lord, thank You for showing me that. It is the number of lessons learned and the lessons that I learn from others, that makes me wiser and stronger. I thank You for molding me through this process. Thank You for showing me the way and knowing that I may stray from Your path from time-to-time, but that my heart and mind are never separate from You. Knowing me as You do Lord, You always let me come home humbled. After each experience, I return a little wiser. Thank You, Father, for loving me that much. Amen.

SPEAK YOUR TRUTH

Say the words below and write beside them your truth. You can also use the workbook to write your responses.

- I Feel...
- I Am...
- I Believe...
- I Am Grateful For...
- I Will Improve...
- I Am Proud of Myself Because...

I Will Stay Out of My/God's Way By…
Today I Will Focus More on…
And Focus Less on…
Today I Will …

GO DEEPER!
Please refer to **Day 71** in the workbook.

NOTES

Day 72: What You Seek, You Will Find

"If you search for good, you will find favor; but if you search for evil, it will find you!"

—Proverbs 11:27 NLT

What we look for we find. I have learned this repeatedly. Yet this wisdom still has not penetrated my mind and heart deep enough. I still struggle to realize that even when we ask God to show us the truth, we don't need to dig looking for the root. Especially if we are not prepared for what awaits us. We are to wait on the Lord to reveal all things, all truths, and to prepare us for what lies ahead.

Wanting the truth doesn't mean searching for evil. But when you expect to find evil, then understand it will definitely find you. It will seek to destroy your spiritual fabric. Ask God to free you of the torment. Ask God to keep your focus on Him, not everyone else.

Only in God can we find freedom, comfort, and unconditional love. I pray for each of you today. That only good comes your way. That through your walk with God you can fight off evil and walk without curiosity to search for it!

PRAYER

Father, I need You today. I need to keep my focus on You. My fears are clouding my judgment—where I should be I'm not, and where I shouldn't be I am. I know that I am under attack by the enemy, by mortal mind, trying to convince me that lies are truth and truth are lies. My heart aches Lord because I want to hear only Your voice but I have allowed another to replace Your warm words. I want to do right Lord, I want to live right, and live by Your principles, not mans'. I don't want to live a double life, God.

Father help me find my way back to You. Help me to search only for good so that I may find only favor and goodness each day. Help me to know You, Father. Help me to see and feel Your protection; to know that You will never put me through more than I can handle. Let me see Jesus' strength so that I may use his examples, and remember his words to guide me in troubled times. Humbly I ask this of You Father. Amen.

SPEAK YOUR TRUTH

Say the words below and write beside them your truth. You can also use the workbook to write your responses.

> I Feel...
> I Am...
> I Believe...
> I Am Grateful For...
> I Will Improve...
> I Am Proud of Myself Because...
> I Will Stay Out of My/God's Way By...
> Today I Will Focus More on...
> And Focus Less on...
> Today I Will ...

GO DEEPER!

Please refer to **Day 72** in the workbook.

NOTES

Day 73: Finish What You Start

"To learn, you must love discipline; it is stupid to hate correction."

—Proverbs 12:1 NLT

Let's focus on being disciplined. We have a tendency to have attention deficit as we jump from one thing to the next, one person to the next. Never finishing what we start—never trying to see things through to the end. Now don't say, *"Wait, Natasha, you told us the other day that we have to walk away from some things. You said that not everything has to be seen through to the end"*. You're correct. I did say that. Let's look at the context. Don't stay in bad situations. Don't keep chasing something God has told you to leave alone. That is not the context I'm speaking of today. If we don't like how something feels at that very moment we bail. We are quick to abandon goals and ideas because the process isn't as easy as we thought.

That is the mind of an undisciplined person. It doesn't matter if you're disciplined in one area and not in another. You should strive to be disciplined in all areas of your life. Not perfect, disciplined. You should also be open to correction from those with the wisdom to help you to redirect your path. You should be asking God to stop you and correct you when you're wrong. This applies to your health, fitness needs, love life, and career. Yes, this also means discipline with housekeeping and car maintenance. Anything and anywhere you're only partially committed. Stop yourself and commit to living right—right now! Dig deep. No one said this would be easy. Will you join me today in the quest for complete discipline in every aspect of our life?

PRAYER

Father today I want to focus on being more disciplined. I don't want to wait until next Monday or the New Year, I want to start today. I want to be focused on starting and finishing a task. Not being sidetracked by other more interesting tasks or things. I want to be focused on getting the job done. Not postponing it or later delegating it to someone else once I've grown tired of the work. I don't want to put off for tomorrow what can be done today. I also want to restructure my personal life.

I understand that it takes discipline to make all things work the right way, at the right time. If it's worth it, then I should work hard for it. I should never let my thinking be that it will always be there waiting. Or ponder the possibility of something better waiting around the corner. What You put before me Lord is what I need to focus on. With discipline, I can give my best and do my best to make things work the right way. I pray for the strength to remain focused and determined. I pray for enlightenment to see that correction is necessary to be a disciplined person. In Jesus' name, I pray. Amen.

SPEAK YOUR TRUTH

Say the words below and write beside them your truth. You can also use the workbook to write your responses.

> I Feel...
> I Am...
> I Believe...
> I Am Grateful For...
> I Will Improve...
> I Am Proud of Myself Because...

I Will Stay Out of My/God's Way By...
Today I Will Focus More on...
And Focus Less on...
Today I Will ...

GO DEEPER!

Please refer to **Day 73** in the workbook.

NOTES

Day 74: Leave Your Worries Behind...

"Worry weighs a person down; an encouraging word cheers a person up."

—Proverbs 12:25 NLT

Today I want you to leave your worries behind you. You have enough baggage. Your worries tell God that you doubt His ability to provide what you need and in time. What we fail to realize is that God knows all, sees all and has the answer to everything long before it becomes our reality. Let go of your worries. Just breathe and tell yourself, *"This is not my battle to be won"* and then surrender to God your cares and worries.

Surrender before you see His work. Surrender before your prayers are answered. You must first surrender, then watch God's work unfold before you. I hope my words have cheered you up. I hope your surrender will fill you until your cup runneth over. Have a blessed day. Thank God for making it through the day, and pray for another sunrise tomorrow. Say a prayer for your family members and friends, those living here with us, and those who have passed on. God bless you!

PRAYER

Father, I just want to say thank You for bringing a calming peace over me. I want to thank You for that extra blessing that came in right on time, which made my worry and cares to disappear. Thank You for sending the angel who pointed me in the right direction. And the person who shared encouraging words that lifted my spirits and made my burdens seem invisible.

Thank You for showing me the need for patience, and prayer while I wait for You to reveal my truths. Thank You for humbling me so that I may be more receptive and appreciative of my blessings, and not taking them for granted. Father when I think of You and Your love I smile. I smile because the feeling of completeness consumes me. I smile because with You I know true love. Thank You for loving me Lord. I love you. Amen.

SPEAK YOUR TRUTH

Say the words below and write beside them your truth. You can also use the workbook to write your responses.

> I Feel...
> I Am...
> I Believe...
> I Am Grateful For...
> I Will Improve...
> I Am Proud of Myself Because...
> I Will Stay Out of My/God's Way By...
> Today I Will Focus More on...
> And Focus Less on...
> Today I Will ...

GO DEEPER!

Please refer to **Day 74** in the workbook.

NOTES

Day 75: The Enemy is About Smoke and Mirrors

But some of them said, "He drives out demons by Beelzebul, the ruler of the demons!" And others, as a test, were demanding of Him a sign from heaven. Knowing their thoughts, He told them: "Every kingdom divided against itself is headed for destruction, and a house divided against itself falls. If Satan also is divided against himself, how will his kingdom stand? For you say I drive out demons by Beelzebul. And if I drive out demons by Beelzebul, who is it your sons drive them out by?

For this reason they will be your judges. If I drive out demons by the finger of God, then the kingdom of God has come to you. When a strong man, fully armed, guards his estate, his possessions are secure. But when one stronger than he attacks and overpowers him, he takes from him all his weapons he trusted in, and divides up his plunder. Anyone who is not with Me is against Me, and anyone who does not gather with Me scatters.

—Luke 11:15-23 HCSB

How can people watch good things happen and question their goodness? I can't recall ever seeing something wonderful happen and think it was the work of the enemy. But time and time again the people questioned Jesus and doubted that his work was by, through, and for God. The enemy is not capable of producing goodness. It's all smoke and mirrors—a trick to make you think life could be better serving darkness over Light. But the enemy never produces Light.

A miracle can never be performed by the enemy. Healing does not come from the enemy. Life is Light and also not a component of the enemy's toolbox. For the enemy merely exists and only exists because God allows it. Existence is not life. It is not living. Existence does not have a greater purpose or a farther journey. Remember that anyone who does good in Jesus's name is with him and not against him. Anyone who performs an act of evil is against Love, Life, Truth, Christ, God, and yes—against you!

DEPRESSION

If you are depressed then focus on taking things moment by moment, not day-to-day. Focus on what's real, right, and true. That grey area is not God. The depression is a state of existence that drains Light from you. God wants you to see, embrace, and live in the Light. It has to be a solid partnership between you and God, to realign you to your rightful place and space.

CLUTTERED LIFE

When you realize your home and car is cluttered and messy, that is not God, for God does not do clutter and chaos. When you are overweight from over-consumption and lack of exercise—that isn't a healthy life with God. That's merely existing in a state of limbo. Stressed out, beat down, worn out—that's not God—that's the enemy you are catering to. God deposits energy and fuel, He never withdraws it. The enemy will overdraft your spiritual account if you don't guard yourself. Hanging around negative people, being negative, whining, and complaining, that's not God. Always yapping about woulda, coulda, shoulda—that's not God. That's not Christ-like. That's you giving in to the enemy.

THE ENEMY VERSUS CHRIST

Being the victim—that's the enemy. Helplessness is the enemy. Procrastination is the enemy. Laziness is the enemy. Making excuses—yep, that's the enemy. Lack of hope definitely isn't God, because God is hope. Waiting for someone else to do what God has equipped you to do, but you are too afraid—that's a double whammy of the enemy. Because that totally goes against Jesus's teachings.

Finding solutions—that's Christ. Seeing only the problems—that's the enemy. Seeing opportunities—that's Christ. Trying to always take the easy route because you're too lazy to put in the work—that has the enemy written all over it. The words Can't and Impossible are the words frequently churned into your mind by the enemy. God always makes a way. You just have to ask and be prepared to receive—without procrastination, doubt, or fear. You must put in work, stop being passive, and merely existing in life as a consumer. Start living and start producing, in Jesus's name.

PRAYER

Father, I never want to be separated from Your Kingdom. I desire my core and foundation to be totally filled by Your Light. I want to be whole within You, never divided, lost, dazed, or confused. You sent Jesus to show me the way. Please stop me before I dare question or doubt. Correct my thinking.

Correct my steps. Correct my speech. You know that it is fear and that I am rebuilding my faith to the level it was in the womb—never wavering. I choose to walk as a believer and follower of Christ. I understand the responsibility that I assume, as this is not an easy task or journey—nor is it meant to be. Each step I take is with the belief that You have already laid the pathway before me. I thank You, Father. In Jesus' name. Amen.

SPEAK YOUR TRUTH

Say the words below and write beside them your truth. You can also use the workbook to write your responses.

I Feel...
I Am...
I Believe...
I Am Grateful For...
I Will Improve...
I Am Proud of Myself Because...
I Will Stay Out of My/God's Way By...
Today I Will Focus More on...
And Focus Less on...
Today I Will ...

GO DEEPER!

Please refer to **Day 75** in the workbook.

NOTES

Day 76: Check Yourself Before You Wreck Yourself

"For everyone who exalts himself will be humbled, and the one who humbles himself will be exalted."

—Luke 14:11 HCSB

It doesn't matter your title, position, level of education, or balance in your bank accounts. The size and value of your financial portfolio, vehicle, and home doesn't matter—you can lose it all. You are only as great as God makes you. Anything else is just in your limited mind and imagination. Check yourself.

PRAYER
Father may I always remain a humble servant, never thinking more of myself, but always grounded and centered in You. Amen.

SPEAK YOUR TRUTH
Say the words below and write beside them your truth. You can also use the workbook to write your responses.

I Feel...
I Am...

I Believe...
I Am Grateful For...
I Will Improve...
I Am Proud of Myself Because...
I Will Stay Out of My/God's Way By...
Today I Will Focus More on...
And Focus Less on...
Today I Will ...

GO DEEPER!

Please refer to **Day 76** in the workbook.

NOTES

Day 77: Want to Make God Laugh? Tell Him Your Plans

"We can make our own plans, but the LORD gives the right answer."

—Proverbs 16:1 NLT

I saw this verse and smiled. There's a quote that I've heard for many years that I recently discovered was attributed to the wrong person. The humorous, yet enlightened quote is from legendary entertainer Woody Allen. He said, *"If you want to make God laugh, tell Him your plans"*. This is true today as it was yesterday. Whether you like and admire Mr. Allen, or not, is irrelevant. It's the quote that I'm focused on because those words are no or less true if Mr. Allen said them or not. The reality is, we can plan until we're blue in the face—if God does not see fit to answer you then you will wait. Waiting could mean actually receiving a better blessing than you ever imagined. So don't get upset or frustrated if something doesn't happen as planned.

Smile, because you know God has something better in-store. Or He's delaying your plans because you're not ready for all or part of what you're trying to create. As you navigate through today, be sure to enjoy it. I hope that you are spending it doing something rewarding and nurturing. Hopefully, you're spending it with a loved one or doing something loving for someone. Hopefully, you're not spending it concerned about the past, future, or what you can't control today. Just be present with God, with love, with your loved ones, and doing something that you love.

PRAYER

Father, thank You for showing me that I can plan all that I want, but only You will make things happen, and only on Your time. Thank You Father for this experience because I am learning patience. I am being humbled in my understanding that I am Your servant, not the other way around. No book or person can give me the full answer to my problems. Only through my connection and relationship with You is that possible. Only in my walk with You Lord will You reveal the right answer. Only when I am silent and receptive will I see and hear what You have planned for me. Only then will Your Word make sense, connect and speak to me, and free me to heal and be closer to You.

Father free me from the boundaries and restrictions of calendars. Free me from the false perception of clocks and what time represents. Free me from placing time restrictions on reaching greatness. Free me from thinking that I can only do something by a certain date. There is no time in Your Mind. Time is relative to Your timetable. Something that would appear to take five years to achieve can be done in five months or even five days. While something that one would rush to complete in six years could take sixteen. It is about us being present with You; waiting for You. Thank You, Father. Keep showing me; keep molding me, Father. In Your Son Jesus' name, I humbly pray. Amen.

SPEAK YOUR TRUTH

Say the words below and write beside them your truth. You can also use the workbook to write your responses.

> I Feel...
> I Am...
> I Believe...
> I Am Grateful For...
> I Will Improve...

I Am Proud of Myself Because...
I Will Stay Out of My/God's Way By...
Today I Will Focus More on...
And Focus Less on...
Today I Will ...

GO DEEPER!

Please refer to **Day 77** in the workbook.

NOTES

Day 78: Be in Alignment

The Pharisees, who were lovers of money, were listening to all these things and scoffing at Him. And He told them: "You are the ones who justify yourselves in the sight of others, but God knows your hearts. For what is highly admired by people is revolting in God's sight.

—Luke 16:14-15 HCSB

God knows our hearts. No matter what you profess, He knows the Truth. Align with Him or be realigned.

PRAYER
Father, may I always be aligned with You. Amen.

SPEAK YOUR TRUTH
Say the words below and write beside them your truth. You can also use the workbook to write your responses.

I Feel...
I Am...
I Believe...
I Am Grateful For...
I Will Improve...

I Am Proud of Myself Because...
I Will Stay Out of My/God's Way By...
Today I Will Focus More on...
And Focus Less on...
Today I Will ...

GO DEEPER!
Please refer to **Day 78** in the workbook.

NOTES

Day 79: We Have All Sinned

And Samuel said unto the people, Fear not: ye have done all this wickedness: yet turn not aside from following the LORD, but serve the LORD with all your heart; Only fear the LORD, and serve him in truth with all your heart: for consider how great things he hath done for you.

—1 Samuel 12:20, 24 KJV

We have all sinned. We have done things to dishonor our Father. In the book of Samuel, we read of clearing our hearts and minds to focus us on serving and loving God fully and unconditionally. Then we can and will be great servants and ambassadors for His Kingdom. We must know and respect His power and authority over us and over the universe. We must not take for granted what He has done for us. Nor should we have a selfish expectation that whatever we pray for we will receive. God determines our wants and our needs, what we receive. He has the last and ultimate say on what we receive.

It is through our loyal servitude that we receive more as we give more. As we trust Him more, our faith in Him is unwavering, and our expression of Him is perfect. Let us let go of what we did wrong yesterday. We have asked for forgiveness, and now we should never do it again. And never come close to doing it again. Or slyly committing a similar sin, but trying to convince ourselves that it "isn't the same." We must never step outside of the realm of God's light for one moment. Intentionally stepping outside of the light, then returning, expecting blessings, is most disrespectful. Let us walk in His light and be the sunshine that nurtures all, heals all, and represents all that God is—perfection! God bless you this day and every day. Walk in the light.

PRAYER
Father-Mother God, oh how I am filled with gladness and joy to serve as Your ambassador. My mistakes and sins have been forgiven by You Lord, and I humbly thank You. Yesterday I said that I want to study Your Word more throughout the day. Not just once a day, not just on Sunday or at mid-week service. I want to serve You in truth and with my whole heart. I want You to have all of me. I am never separated from You Father. You have blessed me in more ways than I can count Lord and I am eternally grateful to You. I will never stop praising You. I will never stop seeing You as my heavenly Father-Mother. You are love and You are loved by me. Thank You, God, for always loving me. Amen.

SPEAK YOUR TRUTH
Say the words below and write beside them your truth. You can also use the workbook to write your responses.

> I Feel...
> I Am...
> I Believe...
> I Am Grateful For...
> I Will Improve...
> I Am Proud of Myself Because...
> I Will Stay Out of My/God's Way By...
> Today I Will Focus More on...
> And Focus Less on...
> Today I Will ...

GO DEEPER!
Please refer to **Day 79** in the workbook.

NOTES

Day 80: Because of Your Faith, Some Will Plot

Then a large crowd of the Jews learned He was there. They came not only because of Jesus, but also to see Lazarus the one He had raised from the dead. Therefore the chief priests decided to kill Lazarus also because he was the reason many of the Jews were deserting them and believing in Jesus.

—John 12:9-11 HCSB

The chief priests were on a mission to protect their personal interests. They weren't going to stop until they were satisfied that they were no longer at risk of losing everything they valued. That meant killing Jesus, Lazarus, and anyone else who stood in their way. Anyone and anything that could cause disruption to the status quo and to their way of living had to go.

There are people and forces in the world, who don't want others to be happy, enlightened, and empowered. Especially if it means disrupting a status quo or planned order. These people and forces serve darkness and the enemy, whether they believe it or admit it. It is truth.

Anytime someone intentionally sets out to block the blessings of others, they are working on behalf of the enemy and not for God. Jesus was a direct threat thousands of years ago, and he still is a threat to those who choose darkness over Light. You cannot both love and hate, and find balance within. You cannot hate and find harmony, You cannot tell lies or deceive, and be at peace, or even be of God. You cannot cheat on your spouse/significant other and understand love, or truly give love. You cannot steal from others and live a fulfilled life. You cannot help others until you have a true heart of giving and service. If you dwell on the past then your present is tarnished and your future is bleak. If you only focus on tomorrow, then you have learned nothing. If you cannot forgive, you will never be forgiven. Protect yourself. Pray. Walk right.

PRAYER
Father, I understand that the closer I get to You, the more I begin to walk like Jesus. The more I try to serve the least of Your children, the more I will be attacked by the enemy. Protect me, Father. Shield me from attack. Show me how to walk swiftly through the darkness without taking on or being impacted by the negative "funk". May I have a closer relationship with the Holy Spirit so that I see and hear all that You have planned for me, and all that is needed for me to fulfill my purpose. I humbly pray these things as Your loving servant. Amen.

SPEAK YOUR TRUTH
Say the words below and write beside them your truth. You can also use the workbook to write your responses.

> I Feel...
> I Am...
> I Believe...
> I Am Grateful For...
> I Will Improve...
> I Am Proud of Myself Because...
> I Will Stay Out of My/God's Way By...
> Today I Will Focus More on...
> And Focus Less on...
> Today I Will ...

GO DEEPER!
Please refer to **Day 80** in the workbook.

NOTES

Day 81: His Grace is Upon You

"The grace of the Lord Jesus be with all. Amen."

—Revelations 22:21 ESV

Let Jesus show you the way. Pray for him to connect with you, to touch your heart and mind— to be the guiding light to our Father. Embrace him. Trust him. Love him. He loves us. Each one of us. His grace is upon all of us, not some of us—not just believers but also non-believers. He is loving and patiently waiting for us. Let's join him.

PRAYER

Father, Your Son's grace is with Your children because of You. Thank You for bringing him here. Through You, he proved Your omnipotence, omniscience, and omnipresence. You have placed him in our lives to show us the way, the truth, and the light. Jesus is the purest example and proof that death, as we know it, is unreal. Jesus shows us that after we are done faithfully serving You here on Earth, our place in Your kingdom will be secured as Your eternal ambassadors. Thank You, Father. In Your Son's name, I pray and praise. Amen.

SPEAK YOUR TRUTH

Say the words below and write beside them your truth. You can also use the workbook to write your responses.

> I Feel…
> I Am…
> I Believe…
> I Am Grateful For…
> I Will Improve…
> I Am Proud of Myself Because…
> I Will Stay Out of My/God's Way By…
> Today I Will Focus More on…
> And Focus Less on…
> Today I Will …

GO DEEPER!

Please refer to **Day 81** in the workbook.

NOTES

Day 82: Value Every Experience Through Gratitude

"...Amen, blessing and glory and wisdom and thanksgiving and honor and power and might, be to our God forever and ever. Amen."

—Revelations 7:12 NASB

Let us be thankful for today. For the yesterdays we remember, and for tomorrows that aren't promised but we are hopeful to see. Let every experience be valued. It is through God's grace and limitless wisdom that we're able to see and experience all that we have, and all that we will. Don't take for granted the small things that seem to just happen, or just be. They are only present and real because of God.

Don't take for granted the vast, thinking that the abundance will always be supplied. We have seen the destruction of the trees, mountains, and water sources. We have also seen the extinction of creatures that used to roam this planet in the thousands. Just because it is present today does not mean that it will be in years to come.

Take the time to appreciate all that is around you, both tangible and intangible. Make the time to spend with family, friends, associates, and neighbors. Today, right now, this very second we are here but we do not know what comes after this moment.

PRAYER
Father, I thank You for blessing me every single day. I thank You for Your favor and the wisdom to see my way through each obstacle and see each person for their true self. Thank You for Your power to change my situations, to make my crooked paths straight, and my rugged ways smooth. Forever I will be faithful to You Lord. Amen.

SPEAK YOUR TRUTH
Say the words below and write beside them your truth. You can also use the workbook to write your responses.

- I Feel…
- I Am…
- I Believe…
- I Am Grateful For…
- I Will Improve…
- I Am Proud of Myself Because…
- I Will Stay Out of My/God's Way By…
- Today I Will Focus More on…
- And Focus Less on…
- Today I Will …

GO DEEPER!
Please refer to **Day 82** in the workbook.

NOTES

Day 83: Peace

You will keep him in perfect peace whose mind is stayed on you, because he trusts in you.

—Isaiah 26:3 ESV

Do what God wants and receive all the blessings He has waiting for you. Be obedient when God calls on you. Obey the voice that redirects your steps. Pay close attention to the still, small, voice that you hear within. It is God speaking to you. We oftentimes say, *"Something told me to..."* or we call it intuition, or our gut. That "something" is God. The gift of intuition is and from God. My dad used to always tell me, *"Tasha, you always mess up when you don't listen to and obey that small voice within..."* and he was correct.

God doesn't need to yell loudly to get your attention. You can hear His voice when you are aligned with Him, and tune out the other noises and voices. By tuning out the noise you can focus your attention on Him. It is like the sheep who only move to the sound of their shepherd's voice. No other voice can direct or redirect them. They will stand still to other voices. But when they hear the shepherd's voice, then they obediently move. That is how we should be with God. There is a peace that comes from being aligned and in line with God. Welcome the peace within. Breathe in the simplicity of life as He has created it. Submit yourself to Him. Surrender to Him and you will see that the chaos you have and are sinking in, will cease to exist.

PRAYER
Father, Thank You for peace today. Not any peace, but perfect peace that only You can provide. I receive it as a comforting blanket for my heart, my mind, my spirit, and my soul. I choose to focus on Your word today and not my fears. Rid me of doubts about others You have placed in my life. Rid me of self-doubt that haunts me and hinders my growth. Direct my steps, guide, and guard me with Your peace Father. In Your Son Jesus' name Amen.

SPEAK YOUR TRUTH
Say the words below and write beside them your truth. You can also use the workbook to write your responses.

- I Feel…
- I Am…
- I Believe…
- I Am Grateful For…
- I Will Improve…
- I Am Proud of Myself Because…
- I Will Stay Out of My/God's Way By…
- Today I Will Focus More on…
- And Focus Less on…
- Today I Will …

GO DEEPER!
Please refer to **Day 83** in the workbook.

NOTES

Day 84: Your Pride and Ego Will Make You a Fool

"and you will know the truth, and the truth will make you free."

—John 8:32 NASB

This is going to be a deep and revealing message today. I share this because my loving relationship with God and Jesus is no longer a private one for me to keep to myself. If we are to grow and become one with God, to build His Kingdom—we must share our trials, tribulations, and testimonies. That way we can all learn and see God's presence protecting and guiding us.

In or around September 2010 I asked God to show me the truth about a situation. I asked Him to open my eyes and reveal the truth. What I did not truly understand was that this revelation would hurt so bad that it would be hard to breathe, think, or sleep. My body was in pain—but I knew I had to continue pressing forward knowing that it wouldn't last long. For a few months, it felt as though life had been cutting at me like quick slices from a knife, or millions of paper cuts. To find out that my reality was a lie had been so painful to accept. The reality is that I ignorantly believed I was placing God first in my life and in my decisions. When in actuality I was putting myself first. I was putting my wants before the needs God has put His 'stamp' of approval on. As I prayed, those around me told me that I was to wait for God's instruction about what to do. I was not to flee or make my situation worse. I was supposed to sit silently and pray for His message. I had also been counseled to not go deeper because I would be tricked into believing the lie. The lie is not God's reality, nor is it His plan for my life. But I must sit still and wait for Him. That was so troubling to me. It was so painful. I wasn't sure what lesson I was supposed to learn exactly.

I had so many questions: Am I supposed to acknowledge one or all parts that I see presently? Is there more? How will this help me be a better child, steward, and ambassador to God? What is this experience preparing me for? I felt like and honestly, still feel like a fool. Like a naive child who should have known better, who should have paid attention to the warning signs but did not. Am I too nice, too loving, too generous, too giving of my heart? Jesus said to keep our eyes and minds always alert so that we can see when light, as well as darkness, is approaching. I trusted that I was walking next to the light. Then I wondered if I was wrong—or if darkness was seeping its way in to try to overshadow this light I trusted. Or if it was trying to cast a shadow over my light. The truth will make us free. It may not be pain—free initially. But freedom from shackles hurts at first until you've been free for some time. I am still waiting to be free.

I am waiting for the lesson to be fully realized so that I can stop repeating this. I know this is a repeated lesson because the feelings are the same. The messages in my dreams are the same. The messages that come to me throughout the day are the same. I must see and know the truth in total—so that I can move forward on the path that God has for me. I cannot be concerned with the temporal but the eternal. I cannot be consumed with what feels good, but what is of God—and nothing that is of God would ever make me feel the way I do. Let your day be exceptional as God blesses you every second you breathe. There is no greater than God and Jesus. True love and joy only come from a relationship with them. Know yourself so you can know them. I want to thank my mentors and family members that have been a source of support and love. Especially these past several years. I also want to thank my guardian angels. I can't see them, but I definitely feel their presence.

PRAYER

Father, I bow myself to You. The truth I seek does not always feel good once received. You nor Your Son ever said that the journey and revelation of truth would be pain-free. It is my desire to no longer hurt that makes me desire freedom in the truth that is painless. This desire is also slowing down the process of You revealing all to me sooner. Father, I'm torn. I want to know the whole truth and I want to live a life with the least amount of pain as possible. Friction brings the most beautiful diamonds to the surface. The penetration of darkness is the only way for light to shine through. Nothing is easy. Nothing is pain-free. I understand this but it is still something that I struggle with.

So today I pray to You for strength to endure this pain. That as You reveal more in my life that I am made stronger to endure, to walk with my head up and shoulders back. I pray that no matter how many lies I encounter—Your truth will always be known to me. When I've learned my lesson and it's time to move forward, I pray for the courage to do so without resistance or fear. Father help me. Thank You for Your favor. Thank You for Your unconditional love. When I can't rely on a human to love me fully, I know that You and Jesus have, do, and always will. Thank You, Father. In Your Son Jesus' name, I pray. Amen.

SPEAK YOUR TRUTH

Say the words below and write beside them your truth. You can also use the workbook to write your responses.

> I Feel...
> I Am...
> I Believe...
> I Am Grateful For...
> I Will Improve...
> I Am Proud of Myself Because...
> I Will Stay Out of My/God's Way By...

Today I Will Focus More on...
And Focus Less on...
Today I Will ...

GO DEEPER!
Please refer to **Day 84** in the workbook.

NOTES

Day 85: Even Through Fear, Jesus Pressed Forward

"Now My soul is troubled. What should I say — Father, save Me from this hour? But that is why I came to this hour. Father, glorify Your name!" Then a voice came from heaven: "I have glorified it, and I will glorify it again!"

—John 12:27-28 HCSB

Jesus knew that he would be crucified, and face human death. He knew that he had to fulfill prophesy without any missteps or delays. He had to press forward because he had to show the world that we are spiritual beings having a human experience. That in reality there is no death because with God we always live. He had to prove that what was prophesied was the truth and that he was the way to all truth. That's not to say that Jesus didn't have moments of fear and hesitation. The scriptures noted those moments, but they also show how he overcame his fear. Jesus demonstrated what we all can do and can be if we only believe, walk, and keep walking.

PRAYER

Father, I know that what I ask for I should not question when or how I will receive it. I know that what I have been called to do I should not question. I pray that I push past my fears; that I face the future with courage, hope, and faith, knowing that You will always take care of me and direct my steps. Amen.

SPEAK YOUR TRUTH

Say the words below and write beside them your truth. You can also use the workbook to write your responses.

I Feel...
I Am...
I Believe...
I Am Grateful For...
I Will Improve...
I Am Proud of Myself Because...
I Will Stay Out of My/God's Way By...
Today I Will Focus More on...
And Focus Less on...
Today I Will ...

GO DEEPER!

Please refer to **Day 85** in the workbook.

NOTES

Day 86: Relying Upon God

Your conduct must be free from the love of money and you must be content with what you have, for he has said, "I will never leave you and I will never abandon you."

So we can say with confidence, "The Lord is my helper, and I will not be afraid. What can man do to me?"

—Hebrews 13:5-6 NET

Once we come to a point where we fear nothing, other than displeasing God—we will be at the very place He has intended. When we no longer rely on money as our king and solution to our problems—and instead rely on God—we will see our lives as He does. We will know that money is merely a tool, an instrument, but it is not the source of what we desire. We will truly be walking in faith knowing that no matter what situation we encounter He is there. We will never fear poverty, homelessness, illness, death, or life. We will never fear abandonment, being unloved, or being alone.

We will be complete with Him. I am grateful for everyone who connects to me through **BreakingBreadWithNatasha.com**. I am grateful that you find a connection with the messages that come from God's love and light. I hope that this book meets your needs and expectations. Enjoy your day. God bless you.

PRAYER

Father, You have never stopped blessing me. You have always provided me with shelter; never homeless—because my home is with and in You. I know that a house is not a home if You are not the foundation. I know that the money I earn is Yours—and You made those provisions for me. I know that my material possessions are on loan to me by You. I will not be afraid of losing what I have because God, You are my provider. I will fight my fears because I know You will never abandon me. Father help me say and believe with confidence that I fear nothing. In Your Son's name, I pray. Amen.

SPEAK YOUR TRUTH

Say the words below and write beside them your truth. You can also use the workbook to write your responses.

> I Feel...
> I Am...
> I Believe...
> I Am Grateful For...
> I Will Improve...
> I Am Proud of Myself Because...
> I Will Stay Out of My/God's Way By...
> Today I Will Focus More on...
> And Focus Less on...
> Today I Will ...

GO DEEPER!

Please refer to **Day 86** in the workbook.

NOTES

Day 87: Worship God Not Man

Nevertheless, many did believe in Him even among the rulers, but because of the Pharisees they did not confess Him, so they would not be banned from the synagogue. For they loved praise from men more than praise from God.

—John 12:42-43 HCSB

People were more concerned about being banned from the synagogue by the Pharisees than their relationship with Jesus and God. They were more concerned about a physical structure than worshipping the one who brought them life and salvation. They were more fearful of the perceived power that the Pharisees and chief priests had than they were of God's power. How ignorant is that? We do this even today. Wake up. Change.

PRAYER

Father may I always seek, turn to, look for, praise, and honor You in my daily walk. May I never reject, dismiss or deny my place in Your Kingdom, Your son Jesus Christ, or You as my Father. May I never put man before You. In Jesus' name. Amen.

SPEAK YOUR TRUTH

Say the words below and write beside them your truth. You can also use the workbook to write your responses.

I Feel...
I Am...
I Believe...
I Am Grateful For...
I Will Improve...
I Am Proud of Myself Because...
I Will Stay Out of My/God's Way By...
Today I Will Focus More on...
And Focus Less on...
Today I Will ...

GO DEEPER!

Please refer to **Day 87** in the workbook.

NOTES

Day 88: It's Thanksgiving

Continue earnestly in prayer, being vigilant in it with thanksgiving;

—Colossians 4:2 NKJV

Today is Thanksgiving. Well, it may not be the holiday, Thanksgiving, when you read this, but every day is Thanksgiving. Every day is a day to be grateful so we must always thank God for our blessings. Be grateful to have people in your life who truly love you. Not the groupies, leaches, and hangers-on who are only around in good times. Thank God for your family. Even when you have issues with them. You know that when times get tough you can count on them to help you see things through.

PRAYER

Father, I am thankful today for the blessings of life, good health, a loving family, and true friends. I am thankful for a career that is filled with limitless possibilities. Father thank You for showing me that even in loss there is a gain. I bow my head to You humbly thanking You for all that You have done for me—and for all that You still have planned. Thank You, Father. Amen.

SPEAK YOUR TRUTH

Say the words below and write beside them your truth. You can also use the workbook to write your responses.

I Feel...
I Am...
I Believe...
I Am Grateful For...
I Will Improve...
I Am Proud of Myself Because...
I Will Stay Out of My/God's Way By...
Today I Will Focus More on...
And Focus Less on...
Today I Will ...

GO DEEPER!

Please refer to **Day 88** in the workbook.

NOTES

Day 89: Don't Be Confined to One Book

Jesus performed many other signs in the presence of His disciples that are not written in this book. But these are written so that you may believe Jesus is the Messiah, the Son of God, and by believing you may have life in His name.

And there are also many other things that Jesus did, which, if they were written one by one, I suppose not even the world itself could contain the books that would be written.

—John 20:30-31; John 21:25 HCSB

We were given a small excerpt from Jesus's teachings and the testimony of some of his followers. But as the scriptures say above, it wasn't possible to record all of his healings, teachings, conversations, and interactions. We can't believe that the enemy only engaged Jesus less than five times in his lifetime, or even in adulthood. Even that is not possible to track and record. Think about your life each day. Is it possible to record every moment of it and then capture it in a book? How many volumes would that cover? Now consider Jesus's life and his travels. Amazing to consider what we don't know and will never know about our faithful shepherd. But let this be motivation to be mindful of the things we say and do. Because we don't know what moments will be recorded and shared later.

PRAYER

May I learn enough to gain the wisdom needed to do right at all times. To speak up for the voiceless. Walk strong for the weak even when I'm exhausted. And face all Goliath-like situations even when I'm afraid. Let me act immediately when You call on me Lord. Without hesitation, doubt, or contemplation. Move me, Father. I believe in Jesus. I believe He came to Earth to show us the Truth. To show us the way to You, and to prove there are no limits to Your power, reach, or love. I will always believe. I will always believe. Amen.

SPEAK YOUR TRUTH

Say the words below and write beside them your truth. You can also use the workbook to write your responses.

- I Feel...
- I Am...
- I Believe...
- I Am Grateful For...
- I Will Improve...
- I Am Proud of Myself Because...
- I Will Stay Out of My/God's Way By...
- Today I Will Focus More on...
- And Focus Less on...
- Today I Will ...

GO DEEPER!

Please refer to **Day 89** in the workbook.

NOTES

Day 90: Silence The Naysayers

So Jesus told them, "My message is not my own; it comes from God who sent me. Anyone who wants to do the will of God will know whether my teaching is from God or is merely my own. Those who speak for themselves want glory only for themselves, but a person who seeks to honor the one who sent him speaks truth, not lies.

—John 7:16-18 NLT

Jesus made it clear that God, his Father, sent him to teach His Word. It wasn't a case where Jesus was walking around making up things and claiming to be the author of the message. He always gave credit to his Father. His love for all mankind was a reflection of God's love. He healed through God's power. He rid people from demon possession; raised people from the dead; healed the sick, the blind, the deaf, and the mute. Yet he was accused of being possessed by demons. No matter what he did to help—he found himself doubted and under attack. Understand that as you do God's work you may come under attack by doubters and non-believers. Even by believers who are envious of your relationship with Him. As long as your focus is on God, His truth will reveal all—and silence the naysayers.

PRAYER

Father, thank You for opening my eyes to the truth. For showing me how to demonstrate this truth. For helping me to speak to others, leaning on Your word, and not relying solely on my understanding. Father, I understand that the closer I get to You, the more I will be attacked by the "liar" and by those whose eyes are not opened and focused on You. Thank You, Father, for protecting me. Thank You for blessing me. I only want to honor and serve You, and live a righteous life. Show me how I can be a better servant Father. Amen.

SPEAK YOUR TRUTH

Say the words below and write beside them your truth. You can also use the workbook to write your responses.

I Feel...
I Am...
I Believe...
I Am Grateful For...
I Will Improve...
I Am Proud of Myself Because...
I Will Stay Out of My/God's Way By...
Today I Will Focus More on...
And Focus Less on...
Today I Will ...

GO DEEPER!

Please refer to **Day 90** in the workbook.

NOTES

Day 91: Tell The Enemy to Get Out of Your Way

The Lord asked Satan, "Where have you come from?" "From roaming through the earth," Satan answered Him, "and walking around on it."

—Job 1:7 HCSB

The devil is a liar. You must protect yourself from the evil schemes that can get you caught up and taken off the path God has placed before you. Tell the enemy to get out of your way, stay out of your way now, today, and always.

PRAYER
Father protect me, my mind, heart, soul, and spirit. Protect my home, my relationships, and my family. Give me the courage and strength each day to rebuke the enemy and keep it out of my space. In Jesus' name, I pray. Amen.

SPEAK YOUR TRUTH
Say the words below and write beside them your truth. You can also use the workbook to write your responses.

I Feel...

I Am...
I Believe...
I Am Grateful For...
I Will Improve...
I Am Proud of Myself Because...
I Will Stay Out of My/God's Way By...
Today I Will Focus More on...
And Focus Less on...
Today I Will ...

GO DEEPER!
Please refer to **Day 91** in the workbook.

NOTES

Day 92: Get Rest, But Don't Be Lazy

"Love not sleep, lest thou come to poverty; open thine eyes, and thou shalt be satisfied with bread."

—Proverbs 20:13 KJV

Sleep is one step away from the eternal rest of our human bodies. We must use it in our current state as a rejuvenator, not as a way to escape reality or to hide from responsibility. Store up those much-needed hours of rest and then rise to take on a new day— a day of work. Those who choose not to work for a living choose a life of poverty. Even those who are financially wealthy can be spiritually poor. God has no real use for lazy people, so humbly make use of the space He gave you. Make today your best day yet!

PRAYER

Father, I know You dislike laziness. Only those that put in the work reap the rewards of their labor. Keep me focused Lord on my work ethic, getting the job done on time every time, and giving it 100% effort. When You say I have had enough rest for one day, wake me, Father, that I might open my eyes and begin work for a new day. I want to be successful in every aspect of my life, and the only way this is possible is through daily labor. I want to be the best reflection of You Father. In Your Son's name, I pray. Amen.

SPEAK YOUR TRUTH

Say the words below and write beside them your truth. You can also use the workbook to write your responses.

> I Feel...
> I Am...
> I Believe...
> I Am Grateful For...
> I Will Improve...
> I Am Proud of Myself Because...
> I Will Stay Out of My/God's Way By...
> Today I Will Focus More on...
> And Focus Less on...
> Today I Will ...

GO DEEPER!

Please refer to **Day 92** in the workbook.

NOTES

Day 93: Soldier For Christ

Then they returned to Jerusalem from the mount called the Mount of Olives, which is near Jerusalem — a Sabbath day's journey away. When they arrived, they went to the room upstairs where they were staying: Peter, John, James, Andrew, Philip, Thomas, Bartholomew, Matthew, James the son of Alphaeus, Simon the Zealot, and Judas the son of James.

All these were continually united in prayer, along with the women, including Mary the mother of Jesus, and His brothers. During these days Peter stood up among the brothers — the number of people who were together was about 120 — and said: "Brothers, the Scripture had to be fulfilled that the Holy Spirit through the mouth of David spoke in advance about Judas, who became a guide to those who arrested Jesus.

—Acts 1:12-16 HCSB

The remaining disciples watched Jesus ascend. As they stood there stunned and amazed, angels appeared and reminded them that Jesus would return. They told them to stop standing there looking up into the sky. Basically, they needed to get back to work and focused on God's mission that Jesus trained them for. There were about 120 men hanging out one day when Peter decided to stand up and speak about the current situation. He spoke about what Jesus was called to do, and what he challenged them to do. Peter could have sat idly by waiting for someone else to speak up, but he didn't. He knew that they were called to do a job and they needed to get out of the "funk" and out of their own way.

They needed to realize that Jesus equipped them to walk, teach, embrace, heal, and show others God's love. They didn't need Jesus physically walking beside them in the flesh to do it. They needed to remember, teach, and practice his lessons. They were mature enough to finally walk. Where do you see yourself in your walk? Are you ready to stand up and walk without making excuses along the way? Are you ready to stop doubting and analyzing everything? Are you ready to commit fully and to act immediately when God tells you to? Are you ready to be that soldier for Christ, one of God's ambassadors, a true servant? Think about it.

PRAYER

Father, mold me so that I may always have the courage and insight to push past my fears and stay focused on the mission ahead of me. Mold me to always remember that just because I can't feel Jesus' touch does not mean he is not beside me. I want to believe that even when I don't see a solution, You will always bring one my way. Help me to embrace this. Push me away from dwelling on things that won't bring progress and that don't glorify Your name. Mold me to stay upright and transparent, reflecting Your love at all times. In Jesus' name, I pray. Amen.

SPEAK YOUR TRUTH

Say the words below and write beside them your truth. You can also use the workbook to write your responses.

- I Feel...
- I Am...
- I Believe...
- I Am Grateful For...
- I Will Improve...

I Am Proud of Myself Because...
I Will Stay Out of My/God's Way By...
Today I Will Focus More on...
And Focus Less on...
Today I Will ...

GO DEEPER!

Please refer to **Day 93** in the workbook.

NOTES

GO BEYOND: Month 3

DEEPER STUDY

You may not be ready for this step at this moment. Please know that if you ever feel overwhelmed, you can return to this activity at a later date. There are numerous scriptures that mention or have something to do with fear and worry. I can recall, in 2017 writing down about 50 versus. Some you will see referenced in this book. Below are 15 verses. Please use your Bible to find and read them:

- John 14:1
- Philippians 4:6
- Philippians 4:7
- 2 Timothy 1:7
- Psalms 56:3
- 1 Peter 5:7
- Deuteronomy 31:6
- 1 John 4:18
- Psalms 23:4
- Matthew 6:34
- Psalms 118:6
- Romans 8:31
- Lamentations 3:47
- Psalms 112:7
- Psalms 49:5

Choose one or more of the scriptures above that speaks to you. Write them down on an index card or piece of paper—something that you can quickly reference. If you want, you can write them down on several cards or pieces of paper. Then you can have them strategically placed in your wallet, gym bag, car, office, or home.

Several times, throughout the day, read silently and aloud the verses. Continue reciting them until you have them memorized. It may take one or more days. There is no rush. Just be patient, as you take in the words and make them a part of you. Whenever fear or doubt creeps into your mind and attempts to halt your progress, recite one or more of these scriptures from memory. Let those words help to move you from analysis paralysis to positive action.

NOTES

MONTH FOUR:

WHAT DO YOU FEEL?

I pray that from the treasures of his glory he will empower you with inner strength by his Spirit...

—EPHESIANS 3:16 CJB

Are you motivated by the flesh or the Spirit?

PONDER THIS: Month 4

If you have read all or part of the Bible, you have read about the Jews, Gentiles, and Greeks. You may even recall reading in the New Testament about the Proselytes. Can you clearly explain the difference and similarities between each group? Who are the Hellenists, Nations, and Strangers, that the Bible mentions? Jot down your answers below.

Now, journey to the **Consider This: Month 4** section towards the end of the book. Let's see if your thoughts align with the historical and cultural facts.

Day 94: Time Is As Precious As You Make It

Men of Israel, listen to these words: This Jesus the Nazarene was a man pointed out to you by God with miracles, wonders, and signs that God did among you through Him, just as you yourselves know.

Though He was delivered up according to God's determined plan and foreknowledge, you used lawless people to nail Him to a cross and kill Him. God raised Him up, ending the pains of death, because it was not possible for Him to be held by it.

—Acts 2:22-24 HCSB

Through Jesus, God proved that our reality of death is not accurate. God is life and through Him, we have eternal life. Our experience here on Earth is to be appreciated, embraced, and celebrated. While we walk this land we are to express, reflect, and share God's love—with everyone and everything we encounter. We don't know how long we will be here so live life to the fullest, learning and sharing as a respectful steward of God's Kingdom.

PRAYER

Father thank You for reminding me how precious my time here on Earth is, and how precious my relationships are. May I be forgiven for the times I have taken this for granted. May I no longer take for granted what You have blessed me with. As a believer and follower of Christ, I pray to You. Amen.

SPEAK YOUR TRUTH

Say the words below and write beside them your truth. You can also use the workbook to write your responses.

> I Feel…
> I Am…
> I Believe…
> I Am Grateful For…
> I Will Improve…
> I Am Proud of Myself Because…
> I Will Stay Out of My/God's Way By…
> Today I Will Focus More on…
> And Focus Less on…
> Today I Will …

GO DEEPER!

Please refer to **Day 94** in the workbook.

NOTES

Day 95: You Are Saved By The Gospel

Now brothers, I want to clarify for you the gospel I proclaimed to you; you received it and have taken your stand on it.

You are also saved by it, if you hold to the message I proclaimed to you — unless you believed for no purpose.

—1 Corinthians 15:1-2 HCSB

May those who believe be saved. May those who are unsure find what they are looking for. May those who are deceptive in their walk be forgiven.

PRAYER
Father, I pray to always be a person of my word. That my integrity is unshakable, and my loyalty to You is unquestionable. Amen.

SPEAK YOUR TRUTH
Say the words below and write beside them your truth. You can also use the workbook to write your responses.

I Feel...
I Am...
I Believe...
I Am Grateful For...
I Will Improve...
I Am Proud of Myself Because...
I Will Stay Out of My/God's Way By...
Today I Will Focus More on...
And Focus Less on...
Today I Will ...

GO DEEPER!
Please refer to **Day 95** in the workbook.

NOTES

Day 96: Jealousy is Like Cancer

"A peaceful heart leads to a healthy body; jealousy is like cancer in the bones."

—Proverbs 14:30

Jealousy eats away at us. It tears us down until nothing is left but a shell. Although we ask God to reveal the truth to us, we should not take this revelation to be our signal to react. But rather to let God handle our issues. God shows us the truth. Our faith in Him must be strong enough to trust that He will never allow us to be harmed in His light. He will always take care of our needs. He will always remove toxic people from our lives. He will remove those who serve as distractions and fuel for our jealous tendencies. It is when we become jealous that we slither over to darkness like snakes.

Waiting and anticipating the chance to attack. It is jealousy that creates mania inside of our minds. It grows so rapidly that before we know it we are doing and saying things that we would never imagine. We want something so bad that we don't realize that we are pushing ourselves farther away from God's light. We find ourselves moving closer to darkness. God is to be our sole provider of happiness, joy, comfort, and love. Through Him, we connect with others.

Through Him, we receive our ultimate riches that no man can provide. We must walk in and of Him, refusing to allow that feeling of jealousy to creep into our minds and hearts. We should not run cold with the venom in our veins. It would cause us to spend our sleeping moments plotting. And our waking moments executing these plans. Instead, our hearts should be warmed by God's love.

We should see Him in our eyes. We should see Him in the smiles of babies. We should feel His presence and know that only our actions limit our connection to Him. We are what stands between us and our destiny in God's kingdom. Don't let the flesh rule you and ultimately destroy your essence. Let our hearts be at peace—with God!

PRAYER

Father this week is a week where strength and wisdom are drawn from Proverbs. The shortest passages hit home the hardest sometimes. This is a week for hard-hitting scriptures. Thank You for humbling me, Father. Thank You for always revealing the truth even when I'm scared to see the reality. Thank You for bringing me peace in moments of chaos. Father, I want a peaceful heart so that I may live a long, healthy life—serving You and Your children. Humbly I pray for Your guiding light. Amen.

SPEAK YOUR TRUTH

Say the words below and write beside them your truth. You can also use the workbook to write your responses.

- I Feel…
- I Am…
- I Believe…
- I Am Grateful For…
- I Will Improve…
- I Am Proud of Myself Because…
- I Will Stay Out of My/God's Way By…
- Today I Will Focus More on…
- And Focus Less on…

Today I Will ...

GO DEEPER!
Please refer to **Day 96** in the workbook.

NOTES

Day 97: Abundance Through Obedience

And Elisha said unto her...what has thou in the house? And she said, nothing but a pot of oil. Then he said, Go all over and borrow vessels from all your neighbors, even empty vessels...and pour oil into them and put aside the full ones....And it came to pass, when the vessels were full that she told her son bring me a vessel. And he said there are no more. Then she told the man of God. And he said, Go, sell the oil, and pay your debt, and you and your children keep the rest.

—II Kings 4:2-4,6-7 NJV

We must be humble to see, and willing to follow, precisely what has been instructed of us. God expects our obedience, no deviation. Imagine if the widow had dismissed Elisha's directives. Imagine if she just scoffed and laughed off what he instructed her to do. Imagine if all she saw was lack. What if she allowed her pride and ego to take over and she said, "I'm not about to go and borrow vessels from my neighbors. I don't want them in my business. What goes on in this house, stays in this house, and I don't need my nosey neighbors knowing what I do and don't have." Imagine if she took that position.

When the vessels were full and she told her son to bring another one, and he told her there weren't anymore, imagine if she walked around enraged because she had no way of repaying her neighbors? Many of us have vessels that we have accumulated that could be sold to pay our debts and take care of our families. Yet we're spiritually blind. We're too consumed by the chaos. Our pride and ego are too strong. We have allowed our fear to appear to be greater than our God.

PRAYER
Father, as Elisha increased this widow's oil I pray that whatever known and unknown resource that I have, that You show me how to make use of it. As the widow did not question Elisha, please bless me with the courage to not question or doubt You. Amen.

SPEAK YOUR TRUTH
Say the words below and write beside them your truth. You can also use the workbook to write your responses.

- I Feel…
- I Am…
- I Believe…
- I Am Grateful For…
- I Will Improve…
- I Am Proud of Myself Because…
- I Will Stay Out of My/God's Way By…
- Today I Will Focus More on…
- And Focus Less on…
- Today I Will …

GO DEEPER!
When you are ready to go deeper, please refer to **Day 97** in the workbook.

NOTES

Day 98: Repent

Therefore let all the house of Israel know with certainty that God has made this Jesus, whom you crucified, both Lord and Messiah! " When they heard this, they came under deep conviction and said to Peter and the rest of the apostles: "Brothers, what must we do?" "Repent," Peter said to them, "and be baptized, each of you, in the name of Jesus Christ for the forgiveness of your sins, and you will receive the gift of the Holy Spirit. For the promise is for you and for your children, and for all who are far off, as many as the Lord our God will call." And with many other words he testified and strongly urged them, saying, "Be saved from this corrupt generation!"

—Acts 2:36-40 HCSB

We must not only seek to be saved from sin, sickness, disease, death, and evil, we must work each day to work and walk humbly. We must show gratitude for all that Jesus has done for us, and the gift God has given us through Jesus. We must show gratitude to God for protecting and forgiving us. And for redirecting our paths when we needed it most. We expect God's commitment to us but what are we giving in exchange? We give empty promises and sing-songy prayers that we soon forget after we say them. Let's do more beginning today.

PRAYER

Thank You for this day Father. Thank You for bringing me to a point in my life where I can read, study, and practice Your Word. Thank You for bringing people and resources into my life to help me in my walk. May I spend the rest of my days working to be the best servant that I can be, and the servant You expect me to be. I pray to never lose my commitment to my walk, and to Your Kingdom. In Jesus' name, I pray for Your forgiveness of my sins, and for Your protection of my soul, spirit, mind, and body. Amen.

SPEAK YOUR TRUTH

Say the words below and write beside them your truth. You can also use the workbook to write your responses.

I Feel...
I Am...
I Believe...
I Am Grateful For...
I Will Improve...
I Am Proud of Myself Because...
I Will Stay Out of My/God's Way By...
Today I Will Focus More on...
And Focus Less on...
Today I Will ...

GO DEEPER!

Please refer to **Day 98** in the workbook.

NOTES

Day 99: Stretch Out of Your Comfort Zone

So those who accepted his message were baptized, and that day about 3,000 people were added to them. And they devoted themselves to the apostles' teaching, to the fellowship, to the breaking of bread, and to the prayers. Then fear came over everyone, and many wonders and signs were being performed through the apostles. Now all the believers were together and held all things in common. They sold their possessions and property and distributed the proceeds to all, as anyone had a need. Every day they devoted themselves [to meeting] together in the temple complex, and broke bread from house to house. They ate their food with a joyful and humble attitude, praising God and having favor with all the people. And every day the Lord added to them those who were being saved.

—Acts 2:41-47 HCSB

When you truly believe, then you know what God can, will, and is doing for you. When you hang around those who are negative you will take on that energy and sabotage your blessings. When you hang around positive people, that energy becomes a blessing to others. When you give in to fear and forget what God has done for you, you block potential blessings from coming your way. When you walk in confidence and with faith, you can both see and embrace all that God has in store for you. When you are more concerned with receiving than giving, you will always be left empty. Givers always have a cup that runneth over. When you selfishly pray only for yourself, you will find out what loneliness is all about. When you pray for others your heart remains warm. Stretch out of your comfort zone. Believe.

PRAYER

Father, I ask that I may see what You need me to see to survive and thrive in life. Help me to see what I need in my Christ-centered walk, with my family, and in my career. When You open doors of opportunity, I pray that I not only see them but that I am strengthened to seize those moments. I pray that I can discern those individuals You send my way from those who have bad intentions.

Father, free my family from debt. Release their burden so that they might rebuild on a better foundation. Heal my loved ones of any and all inflictions. Restore the minds of my elders who may be struggling with reality, time, and place. Free them from the cloud that keeps forming in their minds so that they might truly enjoy days. Help me to be more financially capable of not just taking care of my needs, but to help those who go without. Only You are capable of doing these things and that's why I am humbly asking You for these blessings, in Jesus' name. I praise Your Holy name. Amen.

SPEAK YOUR TRUTH

Say the words below and write beside them your truth. You can also use the workbook to write your responses.

- I Feel...
- I Am...
- I Believe...
- I Am Grateful For...
- I Will Improve...
- I Am Proud of Myself Because...

I Will Stay Out of My/God's Way By...
Today I Will Focus More on...
And Focus Less on...
Today I Will ...

GO DEEPER!
Please refer to **Day 99** in the workbook.

NOTES

Day 100: Look Inside

I tell you that in the same way there will be more rejoicing in heaven over one sinner who repents than over ninety-nine righteous persons who do not need to repent.

—Luke 15:7 NIV

Turn inside and see yourself. Are you putting off repentance? Are you stock-piling until you are ready to cash in your sin "chips"? What can you admit to doing wrong today, and then ask for God's forgiveness? Who have you lied to or misled? What debts are you not paying and you know that you can at least give a good-faith payment? Who are you coveting? What things are you doing and saying, hoping that God isn't paying attention? Trust me, He is always paying attention, listening, and watching. Just stop, check your heart, and repent. Have an incredible day!

PRAYER

Father, I repent for the sins I have committed today. I repent for justifying the things I did or said. Father forgive me for taking You for granted. For not seeing and acknowledging what You wanted me to see and act upon. For not moving when You direct me. For not loving with my whole heart. For doubting You. I thank You for loving me through it all. I give you the glory. Amen.

SPEAK YOUR TRUTH

Say the words below and write beside them your truth. You can also use the workbook to write your responses.

I Feel...
I Am...
I Believe...
I Am Grateful For...
I Will Improve...
I Am Proud of Myself Because...
I Will Stay Out of My/God's Way By...
Today I Will Focus More on...
And Focus Less on...
Today I Will ...

GO DEEPER!

Please refer to **Day 100** in the workbook.

NOTES

Day 101: Do Your Part

Moses said: "The Lord your God will raise up for you a Prophet like me from among your brothers. You must listen to Him in everything He will say to you. And everyone who will not listen to that Prophet will be completely cut off from the people. God raised up His Servant and sent Him first to you to bless you by turning each of you from your evil ways."

—Acts 3:22-23, 26 HCSB

We are being given an opportunity at salvation. But first, we must do our part here on Earth to spread love, build God's Kingdom, and do as Jesus instructed. We have been given instructions. We have been told what to expect. We have been told what we can do through and with Christ. What choices will you make each day? Who are you sharing the Word with? What non-believers and conditional believers are you sharing the Word with? Spending all your time with believers, impacts the building of God's Kingdom in what way? Building requires more followers. Do your part. Commit.

PRAYER

May we see, know, and act accordingly Father as You desire. Mold me Father so that I can be the person You have called me to be. Protect my loved ones. Shelter them from harm. Build them up and give them strength. Help them to push past obstacles to see Your light so that they can reflect it. Help them so that they can help others. May Your Kingdom continue to grow each day in Jesus' name. Amen.

SPEAK YOUR TRUTH

Say the words below and write beside them your truth. You can also use the workbook to write your responses.

I Feel…
I Am…
I Believe…
I Am Grateful For…
I Will Improve…
I Am Proud of Myself Because…
I Will Stay Out of My/God's Way By…
Today I Will Focus More on…
And Focus Less on…
Today I Will …

GO DEEPER!

Please refer to **Day 101** in the workbook.

NOTES

Day 102: Let Go of the Reigns

I will praise You because I have been remarkably and wonderfully made. Your works are wonderful, and I know this very well...Search me, God, and know my heart; test me and know my concerns. See if there is any offensive way in me; lead me in the everlasting way.

—Psalms 139:14, 23-24 HCSB

Are you sick and tired of being sick and tired? Are you worn out from things not going as planned? On Day 77, I mentioned the saying by Woody Allen, *"If you want to make God laugh, tell Him your plans."* This simply means it doesn't matter what your plans in life God is the ultimate decision-maker. We keep getting in the way and we don't realize it. We keep trying to control our lives and we don't understand that God controls all. We are given opportunities to make decisions along our path. But He is the one to move mountains, calm storms, raise valleys, and protect you while you're in one.

About six years ago, I went horseback riding for about two hours one day. Upon dismounting from a very active and strong-willed horse, I realized that I had cut my hand pretty deep. Probably while holding the roped reigns. That's how life can be sometimes when we try to control things that are stronger than us, or that we're unfamiliar with. We sometimes get hurt. Sometimes we have to learn to lighten up our grip on those reigns, and other times we have to learn to let go.

Years ago, Joel Osteen[6] preached a sermon where he spoke about the dreams that we're believing God to make possible, and the situations that we want Him to turn around in our favor. Mr. Osteen went on to say that we put God in a box and tell Him how, when, and who to use to make our dreams a reality. Are you one step closer to letting go? We can't keep trying to grab ahold like the sides of a pool. Don't get your hand cut like mine (while riding that horse). I hope that today's message reinforces what we have prayed about this year. If you also read my blog, Breaking Bread with Natasha, I hope that today's message reinforces it. I hope that this double-dosage today will help each of us let go and let God.

PRAYER

Father purge from me all that is displeasing to You. Help me to be better, stronger, more courageous, and more giving, loving, and forgiving. Mold me to be a better servant, more patient and understanding, and less inclined to interfere in areas that You control. Open my eyes to see and unclench my fists so that I can let go, and finally, live. In Jesus' name. Amen.

SPEAK YOUR TRUTH

Say the words below and write beside them your truth. You can also use the workbook to write your responses.

- I Feel...
- I Am...
- I Believe...
- I Am Grateful For...
- I Will Improve...
- I Am Proud of Myself Because...
- I Will Stay Out of My/God's Way By...
- Today I Will Focus More on...

And Focus Less on...
Today I Will ...

GO DEEPER!
Please refer to **Day 102** in the workbook.

NOTES

Day 103: Seeking Guiding Wisdom From Advisors

"Plans go wrong for lack of advice; many advisers bring success."

—Proverbs 15:23 NLT

I have said for well over a decade that I am a Woman of Excellence. Expecting nothing less than the best from myself and others. What I discovered was that oftentimes I did not seek out counsel because I felt like I was alone, doing this alone. And that no one would support my dreams. Because in the past my dreams and goals far surpassed what others could grasp. So they discounted them and discouraged me from trying. What I realize now after a few years of settling for just-above mediocrity that this isn't my life.

My life is about excellence. The principle of God that is in each of us if only we tap that well and dig deep to get it. I'm much more than what I'm doing now. God has called me to do more and be more. As His reflection, I cannot merely be content with being okay. I must strive for and achieve greatness in everything and in every way. We are imperfect humans, but as His reflection, we are perfect spiritual beings. So today I declare that no more will I wallow in okay-ness. I challenge myself to push myself past the breaking point as I used to years ago. But this time

God will be my focus and guiding force. The advisers He sent to me will help me to remain focused and committed all the way through.

In 2010 I used to have five advisers, but I was not seeking their wisdom enough. Today I would say that I have two advisors, and still, I'm not seeking their wisdom enough. Today that ends. From now on I will call on them by phone or email asking for advice. So that I can be the most successful person God has intended me to be in every aspect of my life. I want to be successful as God's child.

As a student, entrepreneur, professor, mentor, daughter, sister, grandchild, niece, cousin, and Godmother. And as a future mother and wife. Yes, I believe it will happen again, and this time it will be just as the vision God has given me. Look at your life. How many advisors do you have helping you to reach your personal and professional goals? Seek knowledge. Seek good counsel. God has and will always provide the right people in your life. To help you find your way to the blessings that He has in store for you. Let's do this! Blessings to you. Enjoy your day and be a blessing to someone!

PRAYER

Father thank You for sending the right people at the right time to counsel me. Thank You, Father, for these advisors who help me see not only the big picture but the small, minute details that make up that picture. Thank You for sending them to correct my steps, to point me the right way, to make me think and see, and express Your goodness.

Father, You know the big plans that I have. You filled my mind with the possibilities. But I've realized that I need help, advice, and counsel. From those who know, who have been there and can help me reach those higher levels in my life. Thank You for opening my eyes to the reality that I'm not in this alone. That I have a team that is here to help me see my way to the top of greatness as the child of excellence that I know I am. Thank You, Father. Amen.

SPEAK YOUR TRUTH

Say the words below and write beside them your truth. You can also use the workbook to write your responses.

I Feel...
I Am...
I Believe...
I Am Grateful For...
I Will Improve...
I Am Proud of Myself Because...
I Will Stay Out of My/God's Way By...
Today I Will Focus More on...
And Focus Less on...
Today I Will ...

GO DEEPER!
Please refer to **Day 103** in the workbook.

NOTES

Day 104: "Closet" Christians

When they observed the boldness of Peter and John and realized that they were uneducated and untrained men, they were amazed and recognized that they had been with Jesus. And since they saw the man who had been healed standing with them, they had nothing to say in response. After they had ordered them to leave the Sanhedrin, they conferred among themselves, saying, "What should we do with these men? For an obvious sign, evident to all who live in Jerusalem, has been done through them, and we cannot deny it! However, so this does not spread any further among the people, let's threaten them against speaking to anyone in this name again."

So they called for them and ordered them not to preach or teach at all in the name of Jesus. But Peter and John answered them, "Whether it's right in the sight of God for us to listen to you rather than to God, you decide; for we are unable to stop speaking about what we have seen and heard." After threatening them further, they released them. They found no way to punish them because the people were all giving glory to God over what had been done; for this sign of healing had been performed on a man over 40 years old.

—Acts 4:13-22 HCSB

A "closeted Christian" is afraid. They choose to have a secret relationship with God. Some are conditional believers and followers. Believing and following God based on the conditions in their life. Some are faithful believers and followers of God, but they choose to keep their relationship with Him private. Don't confuse these examples with people who live in hostile territories where practicing their faith could result in torture and death. Most of us could sympathize with this level of fear. I'm referring to people who live in nations with freedom of religion and expression. I lived many years in the closet. People outside of my inner circle did not know what I believed or to Whom I worshipped. For those who had an inkling of an idea, it probably looked like I was wearing two masks.

This was not the case with Peter and John. They chose to live boldly in their convictions, willing to accept whatever punishment or fate that came their way. Not all of us are there in our spiritual walk. However, in a free nation, there should be no question in the minds of those who encounter you if you believe, love, and worship God. They may not know your denomination. But through interacting with you they should at least know that you see yourself as a servant of and for God. They should feel the energy of spirituality flow through you. They should be able to feel and see the Light.

If you are a believer and follower of Christ then you should have no problem letting others know. Both in your personal and professional lives. During your interactions with others, you should never worry about or question if you should mention God. If He is in you then you should be sharing Him with others. If you are His perfect creation and reflection, then the world should see Him through you.

You shouldn't fear the judgment of your faith. I will say this, I can empathize with those of you who struggle with the term and identity "Christian" because of the fragmented nature that has evolved. You don't need to be a part of a group to have your relationship with God, and to exemplify servanthood in your daily walk. For several years I would share some of my favorite Bible verses in the signature line of my email accounts:

| Luke 1:37 | Luke 17:21 | Matthew 4:10 | Matthew 6:34 |
| Isaiah 1:17 | Proverbs 21:5 | Proverbs 21:30 | Proverbs 31:10-31 |

On my social media sites, I proclaim myself as a change agent through God and a servant leader. I don't care if someone is offended or uncomfortable. That is between them and God. I'm a servant and I'm here to share what God calls on me to share. I used to be nervous about being open about my beliefs. I didn't use to like having conversations about religion and spirituality. Just like I still don't like having political conversations. But I will engage when important issues need to be addressed. The reasons for my apprehension have always been because of other people.

People are so passionate about and blinded by religion and politics. To the point that they can become belligerent. Even violent about two topics that they have absolutely no control over. I didn't want to get into a debate over which way is the right way to pray—or worship, praise, be saved, be baptized, etc. I didn't want to debate with people about my choice to pray first before considering medical interventions, or opt-out of medical intervention because I was putting my trust solely on God. I won't debate that I've been healed more through prayer than medicine. Just like I shouldn't have to debate and defend my beliefs about:

- The politicians that I vote for and the reasons why
- Women's rights (and that no one should have the right to tell me what to do with my body)
- Gay marriage (and the hate being focused at people who love each other and are being loving)
- The marginalization of Black people and other people of color
- Targeted racism, xenophobia, sexism, and discrimination
- Many other issues

I've matured over the past year to realize something, I don't have to debate or defend. I don't have to explain myself to anyone. I don't have to defend myself. God knows. God guides. God corrects. I don't have to defend Him. I have my own relationship with God and with Jesus, and no one can change that. So I have nothing to fear, be ashamed of, nervous about, or uncomfortable with. I am here to live my purpose, with purpose, and on purpose, as God intends. I'm here to be loved, share God's love, and be loving. I don't need to drill down or wear someone out about Christ. I just need to touch a life, even for a moment—knowing that God always handles the rest. So don't be afraid, ashamed, embarrassed, or nervous about who you are and to Whom you know that you belong. You don't need to be a deep student of the Word to know and share God's love. We share His love and follow Jesus' teachings by being kind, dignified, and considerate. Stand as a proud and confident believer. Be bold!

PRAYER

Father, may I never fear punishment for worshipping You and Your son Jesus Christ. May I never be ashamed of who I am as Your servant and child. With pride and confidence, may I always perform my duties, share Your Word, and testify about Your love. Keep Your name and Jesus's name from ever coming out of my mouth in vain, for I only want to glorify and reflect You. I humbly pray these things today and forever. Amen.

SPEAK YOUR TRUTH

Say the words below and write beside them your truth. You can also use the workbook to write your responses.

I Feel...
I Am...
I Believe...
I Am Grateful For...
I Will Improve...
I Am Proud of Myself Because...
I Will Stay Out of My/God's Way By...
Today I Will Focus More on...
And Focus Less on...
Today I Will ...

GO DEEPER!

Please refer to **Day 104** in the workbook.

NOTES

Day 105: Are You a Dreamer?

For it is God who is working in you, enabling you both to desire and to work out His good purpose.

—Philippians 2:13 HCSB

We have a lot to be grateful for, even when life or Mother Nature hits us with a devastating storm. Each day that we survive is a blessing and we should show our gratitude. Then we should go out and be a blessing to others, and use our gifts and talents to the fullest in honor of our Creator. What if you don't know what your God-given purpose is exactly, what should you do? Pray.

Pray that God reveals them to you and that you have the insight and vision to see it. And the courage to pursue and live it fully no matter your age or perceived limitations. Are you a dreamer? Do your dreams turn into goals that you pursue and accomplish? Or do you simply dream with the mindset that, "*It's only a dream, I could never have or do that?*" We must offer our dreams to God. Allowing God to mold into us the possibilities of achieving the impossible. When we turn things over to God we free ourselves from the bondage of thinking can't and impossible. We allow ourselves to look around and focus on what God wants us to see and embrace.

How can you possibly see what God wants you to see if you're preoccupied looking in another direction? I know that I've been a wanderer, drifter, coaster before. I know that I've dreamed of some big dreams. Even set some goals to achieve these dreams, but I would oftentimes fail to turn them over to God. Nope, I was too busy thinking it all had to do with me and was only possible by my hard work and efforts. Boy was I wrong, and I'm still wrong any time I approach life this way.

What I want and need in life can only be made possible by and through God. He has to allow it to happen. Just like He made it possible for each of us to be here today. God is our Father-Mother. He is our true and genuine life partner. Honor your partnership with Him. We have all been given another chance, another opportunity to live our purpose on purpose. We have all been given another opportunity to set and pursue goals that bring God glory. Let's focus on what God can do to make our dreams and goals a reality. Instead of us focusing on what we don't have, what we can't seem to do, or whatever bad that has happened to us. Let's focus on doing our part to bring Him glory.

PRAYER
Father, thank You for this day, for another day of life, blessings, gifts, and experiences— to learn and grow from. Father, I pray that if I'm wrong about my purpose in life, that You will help me to discover and live it fully in Your honor. I offer my dreams to You because only You can make them come true. Father, I pray that the goals that I have set for myself only bring You glory, and never a disappointment. I pray that the steps that I take make my Lord and Savior, Jesus Christ, proud to be my shepherd. If I misstep Father, please redirect me, because I never want to walk in the wrong direction away from You. Mold me, Father. You know my heart. I want to be the best servant that I can be. In Your name I praise. Amen.

SPEAK YOUR TRUTH
Say the words below and write beside them your truth. You can also use the workbook to write your responses.

I Feel...
I Am...
I Believe...
I Am Grateful For...
I Will Improve...
I Am Proud of Myself Because...
I Will Stay Out of My/God's Way By...
Today I Will Focus More on...
And Focus Less on...
Today I Will ...

GO DEEPER!
Please refer to **Day 105** in the workbook.

NOTES

Day 106: God Is Not Mocked. What You Sow, You Reap.

Don't be deceived: God is not mocked. For whatever a man sows he will also reap, because the one who sows to his flesh will reap corruption from the flesh, but the one who sows to the Spirit will reap eternal life from the Spirit. So we must not get tired of doing good, for we will reap at the proper time if we don't give up.

—Galatians 6:7-9 NASB

I'm grateful to my mother for sending me today's scripture. It encourages me to continue doing good and to continue being loving. It encourages me to continue treating others as I would like to be treated. And how I would want my loved ones treated. This scripture encourages me to always put God first in every decision. With every word, every thought, and all actions. It also encourages me to accept responsibility for my feelings, thoughts, words, and actions. We have been equipped with self-control, and it is only our fault when we mismanage it or toss it out the window.

There is a section in a devotional book published by Freeman Smith LLC that I want to paraphrase. Basically, it says that everywhere we turn we're faced with temptations to behave undisciplined and ungodly. The world we live in celebrates leisure and misbehavior. God, on the other hand, has other plans for us. He never created us for a life of mischief and mediocrity. We were created for greater things. After reading that I had an a-ha moment. It hit me that no matter how much temptation comes my way, mischief and mediocrity are not my calling. So I must be disciplined enough to keep marching forward in strength, rather than be weak and give in to the world.

Except for movies like Se7en, no one can make you or force you to do anything you don't want to do. You choose to cheat, steal, lie, rape, and kill. You choose to be lazy, be a glutton, be mean, be a bully, be manipulative, and any other number of things. It takes more energy to do or say something negative than it does to be godly and say or do something positive. Being negative is draining. It will suck the energy and life out of you. It ages many people. When you are positive your day is upbeat and bright, and no one can rain on your parade. When you are negative you attract more negativity. When you are negative you can easily be drained of reserved energy, and easily be pushed to your breaking point. Ever consider how much effort would have to go into breaking the spirit of a positive person? Ever wonder why no matter what happens to this person they just don't snap? They don't easily go off on people, fall into a deep depression and check out of life, or give up and end their life.

It's God working inside of and through them. A negative person is always looking to be attacked; always thinking that there is a motive to someone's kindness. They think that someone is judging them or think that some people believe they are better than them. They lack peace and struggle with identity issues. They spend so much time trying to shine on their own that they fail to see and recognize that nothing is possible without God. That's why the spotlight quickly turns off of them onto someone positive. A positive person doesn't need to try to shine, they just do. They can enter a room and everything and everyone just lights up. A positive person is comfortable in pure silence. They are okay alone with their thoughts. They control their thoughts. They don't let their thoughts control them.

A positive person feels the need to stay connected to the Light. While a negative person feels the need to stay connected to the chaos and drama of the world. A positive person says "*I love you*," no matter the situation or outcome. A negative person says "*I love you*" and there are always associated conditions. They will always add, "*but*", "*however*", or "*if*" whenever they are displeased. They love you most and show this love only when their expectations are met fully. There are always conditions associated with their love. Conditions you must adhere to if you want to continue receiving this love.

A positive person will see the need to have God first and in the center of their relationship. They will allow Him to guide them to either continue in a loving relationship or walk away from a negative one. A negative person believes that they are the beginning, end, and the center of the relationship. So we all have decisions in life.

Which will you choose? Will you choose to be disciplined or undisciplined? Positive or negative? Self-centered or God-centered?

PRAYER

Father, there is no reason for me not to do the right thing all of the time. There is no justifiable reason for me to make excuses other than I'm lying to myself and thinking I can lie to you. There are no half-wrongs or half-sins in life. So each day I strive to be honest first with myself and then to Your children. I will stop before I contemplate crossing a line that I know I wouldn't cross if I could see Your son Jesus standing near. I will make it a priority to look through the lens of another person before, during, and after a conversation. Each day I will consider that I may be wrong in a decision or opinion. And through prayer, work to realign me with Your Truth.

When I'm attacked, I will not attack back, for the battle is not mine but Yours. Instead, I will follow through with prayer. And not be sucked into the negativity that awaits me. It is my desire to be more like Jesus, and the only way that is possible is to change through growth every single day. In his name and Yours, I pray. Amen.

SPEAK YOUR TRUTH

Say the words below and write beside them your truth. You can also use the workbook to write your responses.

- I Feel...
- I Am...
- I Believe...
- I Am Grateful For...
- I Will Improve...
- I Am Proud of Myself Because...
- I Will Stay Out of My/God's Way By...
- Today I Will Focus More on...
- And Focus Less on...
- Today I Will ...

GO DEEPER!

Please refer to **Day 106** in the workbook.

NOTES

Day 107: You Can't Fool God

A man named Simon had previously practiced sorcery in that city and astounded the Samaritan people while claiming to be somebody great. But when they believed Philip, as he preached the good news about the kingdom of God and the name of Jesus Christ, both men and women were baptized. Then even Simon himself believed. And after he was baptized, he went around constantly with Philip and was astounded as he observed the signs and great miracles that were being performed.

When Simon saw that the Holy Spirit was given through the laying on of the apostles' hands, he offered them money, saying, "Give me this power too, so that anyone I lay hands on may receive the Holy Spirit." But Peter told him, "May your silver be destroyed with you, because you thought the gift of God could be obtained with money! You have no part or share in this matter, because your heart is not right before God. Therefore repent of this wickedness of yours, and pray to the Lord that the intent of your heart may be forgiven you.

—Acts 8:9, 12-13, 18-22 HCSB

You cannot lie, pay, bribe, cheat, manipulate, or hoodwink your way into God's grace, or into heaven. Whether you believe heaven to be a place here on Earth or somewhere in another level of existence, you can't simply access it through prayer and good deeds. It is God who determines whether your heart is pure, right, and just. God knows our hearts. He knows our intentions, plans, fears, and thoughts long before we comprehend them. Your abilities come from Him. Whether it's the ability to heal or help others in different ways, only our Father can bless you with those gifts. The only way to access gifts and use them fully is to free yourself of Y-O-U. Get out of your way. Get out of your mind. Be open fully to God. De-clutter your life, mind, and heart.

PRAYER
May I always remain humble in Your eyes Father. Keep me focused Lord. I pray for strength, vision, courage, humility, and clarity. Let me see all that I need to see, let me see through the veils people wear, and please reveal to me when I'm wearing a veil. Let me see my hypocrisy and help me to make right the wrongness that I arrogantly walk upon. Realign me, Father. Place me back on Your straight path. When my feet begin to turn, I pray that I never stray or become disloyal in any way. As I already have. The pain of my disobedience is embarrassing because I know better but keep doing wrong. Purge out the junk that I carry within me. Everything that is not of and by You, help me to remove and not reclaim. Keep me focused on the mission Father. May I joyfully serve for Your glory. Amen.

SPEAK YOUR TRUTH
Say the words below and write beside them your truth. You can also use the workbook to write your responses.

> I Feel...
> I Am...
> I Believe...
> I Am Grateful For...

I Will Improve...
I Am Proud of Myself Because...
I Will Stay Out of My/God's Way By...
Today I Will Focus More on...
And Focus Less on...
Today I Will ...

GO DEEPER!

Please refer to **Day 107** in the workbook.

NOTES

Day 108: Keep Your Armor and Shield Close

Know therefore this day, and consider it in thine heart, that the Lord he is God in heaven above, and upon the earth beneath: there is none else.

—Deuteronomy 4:39 KJV

I rebuke the enemy who only has relevance when I give it energy. I rebuke the enemy who is only as great as I make it. When I give into fear it is not God that I give the glory, it is the enemy that is fueled. When I invest my money in people, places, and things that promote the message of the enemy, then it is as though I support the enemy. I pray for discernment and clarity to see the darkness that attempts to enter my life. I pray that I see and bypass the trappings in the world. I pray that you keep your armor and shield close to you, protecting you at all times.

PRAYER

Father, I pray that I turn to You for all of my needs. I pray that my worry is replaced with confidence. That my weakness is replaced by strength, and that my fear is replaced by courage. May You always be my source. Strengthen me, Lord. Help me to fight the temptations of the enemy. Amen.

SPEAK YOUR TRUTH

Say the words below and write beside them your truth. You can also use the workbook to write your responses.

I Feel...
I Am...
I Believe...
I Am Grateful For...
I Will Improve...
I Am Proud of Myself Because...
I Will Stay Out of My/God's Way By...
Today I Will Focus More on...
And Focus Less on...
Today I Will ...

GO DEEPER!

Please refer to **Day 108** in the workbook.

NOTES

Day 109: Smile

But I will sing of Your strength and will joyfully proclaim Your faithful love in the morning. For You have been a stronghold for me, a refuge in my day of trouble. To You, my strength, I sing praises, because God is my stronghold — my faithful God.

—Psalms 59:16-17 HCSB

Kirk Franklin said it best in his song, "Smile". No matter what he went through or goes through he's going to smile—out of gratitude. He's going to smile through the pain, loss, and frustration. Through disappointment, betrayal, failure, and more. He's going to smile, smile, smile. I love that song because it reminds me of how awesome God is, and all that Jesus endured and sacrificed. That I have absolutely nothing to complain about. And that life isn't supposed to be easy—it's difficult and requires work, servitude, and sacrifice.

Each day that we open our eyes, we are blessed to experience something new and different than the day before. We have an opportunity to step outside of our comfort zones and be better servants and stewards. Each day we're given the chance to right our wrongs and be a blessing to others. We can also gain more wisdom through our learned lessons. Isn't that amazing? That should encourage us to sing, praise, dance, and express our love and appreciation for God. If you believe, then speak it and share it with others.

PRAYER

No matter what I go through, lose or gain, or what others say, You will always be my God. And I will always believe that Jesus is my savior. I will pray to and praise You during storms and not just sunny days. I will continue to thank You even in my lowest of hours. Because I'm grateful for life and for the experiences I have had so far. I'm grateful for the love received by You. And the love received from family, friends, associates, and even strangers. I love You Father. Amen.

SPEAK YOUR TRUTH

Say the words below and write beside them your truth. You can also use the workbook to write your responses.

> I Feel…
> I Am…
> I Believe…
> I Am Grateful For…
> I Will Improve…
> I Am Proud of Myself Because…
> I Will Stay Out of My/God's Way By…
> Today I Will Focus More on…
> And Focus Less on…
> Today I Will …

GO DEEPER!

Please refer to **Day 109** in the workbook.

NOTES

Day 110: Righteousness

The way of the righteous is like the first gleam of dawn, which shines ever brighter until the full light of day.

—Proverbs 4:18 NLT

Today, just as yesterday, is a struggle to always do and say right. When life seemingly would be easier if we just did and said what we felt the moment we felt it. We must be disciplined to listen to the small voice that guides and warns us. Understanding that it won't always or ever be the loud voice that tells us to *"Just do it already"*. Before we speak we should pray for loving words. Knowing that there is power in the tongue, and an inability to take back what is said after we speak. We should focus on listening more than we speak. As wisdom is gained through receiving, processing, retaining, and learning.

Like dawn's graceful rising and widening, so should our presence and our impact be in the lives of others. Without saying a word, God's light should be visible to all who encounter you. Jesus proved that it is unnecessary to force yourself, your values, or beliefs upon others. People are more receptive to an open door with a welcome sign than they are to being forcibly led. God never forces Himself upon us, just like dawn doesn't just pop up and spring itself on us. Imagine if darkness turned to light like a flip of a switch—it would be traumatic to all forms of life. Just as it would if it went from daylight to night in one second versus several hours. God's creations would suffer from either extreme. We impact our fellow humans in the same way. Especially, when we attempt to force upon them our views of God, and religion, our practices and beliefs, and our self-proclaimed righteousness. Think about how Jesus taught and healed. It was never forced upon others. He never called on people to gather around Him. He allowed people to watch from a distance. They then could approach through their own interests and inquiry. It was left to them to decide to connect, engage, and interact—or not. That is how we should walk through life. Reflect God's Light and watch people gravitate towards it and you.

PRAYER

Father, I know that You have a wonderful plan and purpose for me. I desire to be right and do right by You. I know that this is a constant struggle. As I have to keep my mind and heart focused on You and Your commands, not the temptations of the world. Show me Your ways and teach me to walk righteously before You. Keep my heart warm, and please be the beacon of light that I need to guide me down the right paths. I humbly pray to You in Jesus' name. Amen.

SPEAK YOUR TRUTH

Say the words below and write beside them your truth. You can also use the workbook to write your responses.

- I Feel...
- I Am...
- I Believe...
- I Am Grateful For...
- I Will Improve...
- I Am Proud of Myself Because...
- I Will Stay Out of My/God's Way By...
- Today I Will Focus More on...
- And Focus Less on...
- Today I Will ...

GO DEEPER!
Please refer to **Day 110** in the workbook.

NOTES

Day 111: The Invited

An angel of the Lord spoke to Philip: "Get up and go south to the road that goes down from Jerusalem to Gaza." (This is the desert road.) So he got up and went. There was an Ethiopian man, a eunuch and high official of Candace, queen of the Ethiopians, who was in charge of her entire treasury. He had come to worship in Jerusalem and was sitting in his chariot on his way home, reading the prophet Isaiah aloud. The Spirit told Philip, "Go and join that chariot." When Philip ran up to it, he heard him reading the prophet Isaiah, and said, "Do you understand what you're reading?" "How can I," he said, "unless someone guides me?" So he invited Philip to come up and sit with him.

—Acts 8:26-31 HCSB

Both Philip and the Ethiopian eunuch were open, receptive, and obedient to God. Philip could have questioned the angel. He could have refused to obey the Spirit's directives. The eunuch could have been close-minded and dismissed Philip. Instead, he welcomed him into his chariot to read the scriptures. We need to be more like this example, and less cynical and skeptical. We need to be more open because we never know what opportunities or blessings may come our way.

PRAYER

Father, I pray for faithfulness to act when called. I pray that when You speak that I not only listen but I answer and respond. I pray that when Your angels direct me that I go without hesitation or question. May my faith be unshakable and unquestionable. In Jesus' name. Amen.

SPEAK YOUR TRUTH

Say the words below and write beside them your truth. You can also use the workbook to write your responses.

- I Feel...
- I Am...
- I Believe...
- I Am Grateful For...
- I Will Improve...
- I Am Proud of Myself Because...
- I Will Stay Out of My/God's Way By...
- Today I Will Focus More on...
- And Focus Less on...
- Today I Will ...

GO DEEPER!

Please refer to **Day 111** in the workbook.

NOTES

Day 112: Leasing From God

Jesus said to him, "Away from me, Satan! For it is written: 'Worship the Lord your God, and serve him only.'"

—Matthew 4:10 NIV

There is no room for fixation, worship, or service of anything or anyone but God. We cannot be consumed by our material possessions or the desire for them. We cannot worry about or contemplate what we have or had, what we lost, or gained. Each moment of each day we are told by God, Jesus, and the Bible, that we should be centered around and on God. No, I don't want to lose my car, go bankrupt, or be homeless. At the same time, I am learning to pray and leave things to God. Rather than obsess and still get nothing accomplished.

These material possessions are His, on loan to us. So we should learn to pray to Him and ask Him how He wants to handle His possessions. We should ask Him about the pending late payment or collection notice. Ask how He would like to handle their resolutions. As we are stewards of His possessions—not the other way around.

Worry won't stop the bill collectors, repo man, or banks attempting to foreclose on your property. But your circumstances can change for the better through prayer and unwavering conviction. And through your faith in God's ability to do all and resolve all. God can get rid of the bill collectors, repo man, and foreclosure. He can supply you with the resources that you need to get those debts off of your back. He can help you to silence the enemy who calls you a failure. God can place you in a position where you can provide for yourself and your family. Without added struggle or sacrifice. The blessings, in many forms, will come through disciplined service and worship of God. But we will lose those things if we invest most of our time and energy in the material and not the spiritual.

We will never gain those things we are focused on attaining. The material is and always will be temporary. But the spiritual is everlasting and boundless. I have lost more material possessions than some people will ever have. It was a crushing blow each time. It humbled me. It also reminded me that I put more value on my material possessions than my spiritual relationship with God. I valued things more than I valued Him. Even though I was a steward of those things, I wasn't being a faithful and honorable steward. I was forgetting that everything I thought that I owned, I merely was leasing from God. I also wasn't showing my gratitude on a regular and consistent basis. I had to be reminded that there are no 'things' without Him. There are no luxuries without God. Just as He gives He can take away, and believe it or not, He does both with love. We cannot benefit from Him and then serve another. It is all or nothing.

I choose to dedicate my life to serving God. To work each day to purge my body and my life of impurities. I choose to live transparently for Him so that He may fill me with His goodness—and bless me accordingly. I hope that today's message speaks deeply to you. As we all struggle with the temptations that will always lead us astray, let's not only pray for ourselves, but for each other. Enjoy your day. Reflect on the obstacles that you overcame and how God guided and protected you. Then embrace the possibilities that tomorrow can bring! Think of all the ways that you can be open in service to our Father. Isn't that an awesome feeling?

PRAYER

Father, I will only worship and serve You. I bless Your children through service as Your ambassador. But I serve only You as You are my Creator, Master, Husband, and Father-Mother. I work each day to resist the enemy's plot to tear me down, manipulate me into doing its work, and convince me to destroy myself. Each day I try to watch and control my words, thoughts, and actions. There are moments when I may slip, and say or think something negative, or react negatively. I try to catch myself immediately to make right the wrong. I ask for forgiveness. For those moments when I fail and give in to the temptation of negativity and recklessness.

Father, help me to shield myself with Your light, to protect myself from the darkness. I pray for Jesus's guidance to show me how he consistently rebuked the enemy and forced it to get out of his way. I don't want anything or anyone distracting me from reflecting Your love and light. Touch my heart and mind Lord. Remove all darkness and fill me only with Your light. Amen.

SPEAK YOUR TRUTH

Say the words below and write beside them your truth. You can also use the workbook to write your responses.

I Feel...
I Am...
I Believe...
I Am Grateful For...
I Will Improve...
I Am Proud of Myself Because...
I Will Stay Out of My/God's Way By...
Today I Will Focus More on...
And Focus Less on...
Today I Will ...

GO DEEPER!

Please refer to **Day 112** in the workbook.

NOTES

Day 113: God Opens Our Eyes to Infinite Possibilities

Praise the Lord! Praise God in his sanctuary; praise him in his mighty heaven! Praise him for his mighty works; praise his unequaled greatness! Let everything that breathes sing praises to the Lord! Praise the Lord!

—Psalms 150:1-2, 6 NLT

People say, "God is good all of the time, and all of the time God is good", and I want us to stop and really think about this phrase. God is good, not just a doer of good, He is good, and He is goodness. All of the good things that we receive are from God, conceived by God, created by God, and delivered by God. This is a constant and unchanging fact. There is no other source of good. All goodness comes from God. Then we must go a step farther. We must remind ourselves that God's goodness surrounds us. Even in times of pain, sorrow, loss, and frustration. God is good to us even at our lowest point. God spares us from a lot of things. God opens our eyes to infinite possibilities. Even when in our under-exercised minds, we see limits. Man diagnoses. God heals. Man puts limits. God has no limits. Man fears and doubts. God is all in all. Man stops. God overcomes.

We rush quickly to man for solutions, healing, reassurance, uplifting, and protection. When we should first turn to God and continue to pray and believe. Even when our eyes and minds don't register the blessings coming our way. When we are healed we give praises to man, not God. When you pray over someone and they are healed, it was not your doing, it was all God. Being faced with human death opens our eyes to the beauty of life. That ironically is also a gift from God. Things we took for granted we now fully embrace and appreciate. We mourn not just what we had but also what we could have. We keep both feet in the past and the future, without being settled in the present.

When you hear someone say, "*God is good all of the time*" don't be so quick to respond, "*And all of the time, God is good*". Not without truly and passionately meaning it. If you believe that God is good all of the time, then never a time should you doubt or be angry with Him. If you believe that God's goodness is never-ending and always present, then you should be free from worry and fear. If you believe that God brings you gifts and blessings, then you should never detour from reaching out to Him in prayer. You should never be so quick to seek man's medicine over God's healing touch.

Yes, it's true, God IS good and He is good ALL of the time. Praise Him and share with the world your love for our Heavenly Father. You don't need to be a minister, preacher, pastor, bishop, priest, or other formalized religious leader to serve God through ministry. You don't need a title to share God's love with the masses. You just need to get out there and share! If you are a believer then believe. If you are a follower then follow. If you are both a believer and a follower, then you know what to do—believe and faithfully follow. I love you!

PRAYER

Father, You are Good, and everything good that happens to me or that I receive is because of You. You are Love. I am grateful for the love I receive from You, and through Your children. When times get rough or unbearable please touch my heart to not question You. To not be so overwhelmed that I don't pick myself up quickly and keep marching forward. Strengthen me, Lord, to know You. To remember that I am Yours. That I'm always protected, and always equipped with the tools and skills needed in life. There is no better, greater, stronger, wiser, patient, forgiving, or more loving than You. I love You Father. Amen.

SPEAK YOUR TRUTH
Say the words below and write beside them your truth. You can also use the workbook to write your responses.

> I Feel…
> I Am…
> I Believe…
> I Am Grateful For…
> I Will Improve…
> I Am Proud of Myself Because…
> I Will Stay Out of My/God's Way By…
> Today I Will Focus More on…
> And Focus Less on…
> Today I Will …

GO DEEPER!
Please refer to **Day 113** in the workbook.

NOTES

Day 114: Stop Comparing

Dear friends, since God loved us that much, we surely ought to love each other. No one has ever seen God. But if we love each other, God lives in us, and his love is brought to full expression in us. And God has given us his Spirit as proof that we live in him and he in us. Furthermore, we have seen with our own eyes and now testify that the Father sent his Son to be the Savior of the world. All who confess that Jesus is the Son of God have God living in them, and they live in God.

—1 John 4:11-15 NLT

Not that we dare to classify or compare ourselves with some of those who are commending themselves. But when they measure themselves by one another and compare themselves with one another, they are without understanding.

—2 Corinthians 10:12 ESV

Today, I share two Bible verses. The first speaks of God's love and how it lives within us and is expressed by us. God is within us and we carry the responsibility of choosing each day to either live in the Spirit or the flesh. God does not compare Himself to other gods, feeling inadequate, so why do we compare ourselves to other people? The same Creator of you made me, and He does not make mistakes. Why do we compare our circumstances to other people's situations? Be grateful for the life that you have because it's yours to live. You did nothing to get it or keep it, for it is a gift. Don't squander it.

These daily experiences come with lessons to gain knowledge, and when applied we gain wisdom. You could be in a worse situation, and you know there are plenty of people facing issues that you could never fathom. There is always someone who has it worse than you, so humble yourself and give praise to God for His loving grace. What is meant for you is yours and will be yours. No one said it would be easy or happen as we would like. But God gives us what we need. Getting what you want is a bonus, be grateful, not entitled. We are toughened and strengthened by the journey. We learn to respect the ruggedness and thereby appreciate those moments of smooth, seamless passage.

PRAYER
Thank You, Father. Thank You for all that I am and all that I have. In Jesus' name. Amen.

SPEAK YOUR TRUTH
Say the words below and write beside them your truth. You can also use the workbook to write your responses.

>I Feel…
>I Am…
>I Believe…
>I Am Grateful For…
>I Will Improve…
>I Am Proud of Myself Because…
>I Will Stay Out of My/God's Way By…
>Today I Will Focus More on…
>And Focus Less on…
>Today I Will …

GO DEEPER!
Please refer to **Day** 114 in the workbook.

NOTES

Day 115: Removing Blinders

...maintaining faithful love to a thousand generations, forgiving wrongdoing, rebellion, and sin. But He will not leave the guilty unpunished, bringing the consequences of the fathers' wrongdoing on the children and grandchildren to the third and fourth generation.

—Exodus 34:7 HCSB

There are countless stories of people who have been raised entitled. They believe that they are entitled to do and say whatever they want. We have seen people who feel entitled to abuse their title and role. There are people who rationalize why they hurt others. They justify beating, torturing, stabbing, raping, molesting, robbing, or murdering another person. Think of the aggressors and agitators, that later claim self-defense for their actions.

We have watched people fake remorse, but never actually repent. Instead, they narcissistically focus on how an event has had a negative effect on them. Some people make excuses or blame others for the ignorant things that they have done or said. Some people want to use their age or where they live (or grew up) as an excuse for how they treat others. There are countless examples of people telling lies and spreading hate in the name of God or Jesus. Promoting the enemy's agenda. When someone is being unloving you do not rally around them to sweep what they have done or said under the rug. You are to rally around them and encourage them to do the right thing, and to make right the wrong they have done. You encourage them to stop thinking and reacting for self and to start embracing God's Light. When they don't, you are to pray for them and those that they will encounter. Then refuse to promote, reinforce, and support their negative thinking. Finally, leave the rest up to God.

We are not to be the rioting crowd. Or crazed zealots chasing down and forcing people to conform to our beliefs. Just like we aren't supposed to sit around passively acting as though there is not a battle taking place. The person yelling, "*You're going to hell...*" is as ignorant as someone who does nothing to help this world be a better place.

The person yelling, "*You're going to hell...*" is as dangerous and ignorant as the racist who spews hate. I will always speak up and speak out when I see hate, ignorance, or deception. It doesn't matter if it's an individual or an organization. What you see in the world today should make you want to do your part to help remove blinders from people's eyes. To help them to love others as Jesus loves us. Unless of course, you have no intention of being a soldier for Christ. Just a thought.

PRAYER

I ask for forgiveness for all the inconsiderate and unloving things that I have done and said. I pray for those who speak and act out of ignorance and fear. I pray for those who don't realize that what they say and/or do is harmful to others. I pray for those who feel entitled to live by their own rules, regardless of how it impacts others. I pray for those with an elitist mentality. I pray for those who discriminate, hate, abuse, misuse, deceive, and take advantage of others. I pray for those who say that they won't change because they are who they are and they won't change for anyone. I pray for those who use Your name and the name of Jesus to justify the ugly things that they do and say.

Father touch our hearts and minds. That we might discern darkness from light. Truth from lies. Love from obsession. Love from hate. And the ugliness that comes from racism, bigotry, and discrimination. Let us see clearly those with forked tongues, two-faces, and double-minds. So that we can do our part to help pray for them, re-direct them or steer clear and leave them to You. Father protect us from ourselves. These things I pray in Jesus' name. Amen.

SPEAK YOUR TRUTH

Say the words below and write beside them your truth. You can also use the workbook to write your responses.

> I Feel...
> I Am...
> I Believe...
> I Am Grateful For...
> I Will Improve...
> I Am Proud of Myself Because...
> I Will Stay Out of My/God's Way By...
> Today I Will Focus More on...
> And Focus Less on...
> Today I Will ...

GO DEEPER!

Please refer to **Day 115** in the workbook.

NOTES

Day 116: His Voice

"In all your ways acknowledge Him, and He shall direct your paths."

—Proverbs 3:6 NKJV

There is nothing too big or too small for God, yet oftentimes we doubt Him and ignore His voice. Have you heard that small voice in your head tell you to do something or go somewhere (or not), and you listened and obeyed? Can you admit that there have been times when you disobeyed? I can admit it. Oh, the numbers are too large to count and track. But I've been hardheaded plenty of times throughout my life. The results have always left me disappointed. Don't walk around being disappointed. If you ask Him, He will answer, if you listen He will guide you, and if you obey there are no disappointments.

When I was much younger I asked the question, *"How do I know when it's God's voice and not the enemy's?"* And the answer I received was so logical that I felt silly yet empowered—If it's unloving then it's not God. The enemy will only lead you to paths of pain, embarrassment, chaos, destruction, and failure. God will never tell you to do or say anything that would cause harm to you or others. Let's begin to turn all things over to God. Let's ask Him for our eyes, ears, and hearts to always be open and receptive. Ask that we close our mouths more so that we can hear Him—and then what we say will always be more loving.

PRAYER

Father, thank You for this reminder. I pray that I begin to turn all things over to You both small and large, simple, and complicated. So that I can be free from the shackles I have placed upon myself. There are no limits in Your Mind. I want You completely involved in every aspect of my life. Direct me, Lord. In Jesus' name. Amen.

SPEAK YOUR TRUTH

Say the words below and write beside them your truth. You can also use the workbook to write your responses.

I Feel…
I Am…
I Believe…
I Am Grateful For…
I Will Improve…
I Am Proud of Myself Because…
I Will Stay Out of My/God's Way By…
Today I Will Focus More on…
And Focus Less on…
Today I Will …

GO DEEPER!

Please refer to **Day 116** in the workbook.

NOTES

Day 117: Riding Through Storms

"Be still, and know that I am God!..."

—Psalms 46:10 NLT

On Monday, June 17, 2013, I journeyed home to Atlanta from Oklahoma City, Oklahoma. I was driving a rented SUV. My mother, sister, and cousin were with me. Almost 11 hours into the drive I realized that the GPS had me driving two hours in the wrong direction. I then followed the suggestion to take another route. It conflicted with an alternate route that my cell phone suggested. This new route had me backtrack 45 minutes and detour four hours in a direction that I had never driven. By hour 15 of driving I began to question why I agreed to that route. We entered a strong storm.

We were trying to outrun tornadic activity and now, we found ourselves in the middle of nowhere. Well, it felt like nowhere. I was driving in pitch darkness, with limited visibility. I began praying for safety and reassurance. By hour 17 I knew I could no longer drive safely. But I was able to get us to Birmingham, Alabama, and to an area of recognizable landmarks. I was grateful that my sister, Alexandra, had the courage and strength to drive the remaining two and a half hours. I didn't stop praying until I was snuggled into my bed and drifting to sleep. A 12 to

14-hour drive turned into almost a 20-hour drive. We made it through that trip safely because of God's guidance and protection. He kept me calm (somewhat), focused, and awake. He made it possible for me to see areas that were overshadowed by fog, darkness, and rain. I was so humbled. I am humbled.

PRAYER

Father thank You for helping me with my fears. Thank You for directing me out of darkness, chaos, and lands where I could become lost. Thank You for helping me through complicated situations. For steering me clear of negative people, and for realigning me when I'm being negative. I don't know everything, but I do know that my blessings only come from You. Thank You, Lord.

SPEAK YOUR TRUTH

Say the words below and write beside them your truth. You can also use the workbook to write your responses.

>I Feel...
>I Am...
>I Believe...
>I Am Grateful For...
>I Will Improve...
>I Am Proud of Myself Because...
>I Will Stay Out of My/God's Way By...
>Today I Will Focus More on...
>And Focus Less on...
>Today I Will ...

GO DEEPER!

Please refer to **Day 117** in the workbook.

NOTES

Day 118: You Don't Receive More or Less of His Love

"He made no distinction between us and them, cleansing their hearts by faith. Now then, why are you testing God by putting a yoke on the disciples' necks that neither our ancestors nor we have been able to bear? On the contrary, we believe we are saved through the grace of the Lord Jesus in the same way they are."

—Acts 15:9-11 HCSB

God loves us. We each have our own unique relationship with Him. There is no one human or group who receive more of His love than anyone else. Instead of being fixated on what you think God wants, why not listen to your heart and follow your feet. Step back from judging and instead embrace others. Have an amazing day.

PRAYER
Thank You for loving me. May I never disappoint You or weaken the relationship that we have. Redirect me from ever placing expectations on others that I cannot fulfill myself. Guide me away from judging others. Touch my heart before I speak. Forgive me for the wrong I've done already today. In Jesus' name. Amen.

SPEAK YOUR TRUTH

Say the words below and write beside them your truth. You can also use the workbook to write your responses.

I Feel...
I Am...
I Believe...
I Am Grateful For...
I Will Improve...
I Am Proud of Myself Because...
I Will Stay Out of My/God's Way By...
Today I Will Focus More on...
And Focus Less on...
Today I Will ...

GO DEEPER!

Please refer to **Day 118** in the workbook.

NOTES

Day 119: Your Commitment

Later the Lord chose seventy-two other followers and sent them out two by two to every town and village where he was about to go. He said to them: A large crop is in the fields, but there are only a few workers. Ask the Lord in charge of the harvest to send out workers to bring it in. Now go, but remember, I am sending you like lambs into a pack of wolves. Don't take along a moneybag or a traveling bag or sandals. And don't waste time greeting people on the road.

As soon as you enter a home, say, "God bless this home with peace." If the people living there are peace-loving, your prayer for peace will bless them. But if they are not peace-loving, your prayer will return to you. Stay with the same family, eating and drinking whatever they give you, because workers are worth what they earn. Don't move around from house to house. If the people of a town welcome you, eat whatever they offer.

—Luke 10:1-8 CEV

In this story, Jesus sent out 72 men to help build God's Kingdom. They were supposed to reinforce the pre-Jesus era principles. Those great stewards and messengers before him helped to plant the seed. Jesus came to show and prove how to nurture, grow, and harvest that seed. So that nations could live off of that spiritual fruit forever. Later verses tell of how the 72 returned ecstatic when demons bowed after hearing Jesus' name.

Jesus stated that he watched Satan fall from heaven. So the men should not be ecstatic because some demons bowed down and were defeated. They should be overjoyed at the fact that all 72 of the men had their place in heaven. They did God's work. As Jesus instructed. Without question, doubt, faltering, complaining, or making adjustments to their orders. They were disciplined. They were not greedy or felt the need to move from home to home, looking for a better situation. The metaphorical 'grass' was green enough in the yard they were in—they were satisfied. Can we say the same of ourselves?

Are we satisfied with the place that we have been instructed to go, to live, to work? Are we doing our part with 100 percent effort? Are we showing Jesus and God that we deserve more and greater by being on time, every time, for everything? Or do we arrive when we feel like it? Are we showing Jesus and God that we deserve more and greater by taking care of the things that God has loaned us? Or do we leave things messy, dirty, half-fixed, and worse than when we got them? Are we grateful for the food and clothing that we have? Or are we always envying and desiring better...when we haven't done our part to earn and deserve better? Are we satisfied with those people around us who care, nurture, protect, and guide us? Or are we always looking next door or down the street wondering if there is someone better out there for us?

We have all been given tasks to complete. No questions are to be asked. Upon completion, you will be granted your blessings—rewarded for a job well done. Why are we not committed enough to do our jobs? It is no wonder many of us get written up or fired at work for mediocre job performance, attendance issues, and subordination. We can't do the job that God has commanded, and that Jesus mapped out the steps. So why should we be committed, disciplined, and willing to do an easy job at someone's company? Do you see how the two are tied together? Do you see how this is tied together?

We have to strive and do our jobs with 100 percent effort. No questions asked (unless you have an ethics issue of course). Every single day. While we do our job, we are also doing some of the work that God assigned to us. When we clock out and leave work, we are then devoting the rest of our time to working on building God's Kingdom. Every single day this is our mission. Every single day you are to be a blessing to others. That is how we receive our many blessings. It is a beautiful cycle that nurtures and harvests some amazing 'fruit'.

PRAYER

Father thank You for sending Your Son to us to show us the way to You. He taught us how to be patient, kind, giving, caring, and nurturing. He taught us how to be loving, peaceful, forgiving, and present in the moment. Not concerned with past or future issues because You have already dealt with them. He taught us how to heal ourselves and others through You. But we have strayed a great deal over the thousands of years since Jesus walked this earth. We have devised more substitutions for You and for him, that we are now confused. We might as well be the children of Israel walking around in the forest waiting to prove ourselves again.

Father open our eyes, show us that the way You point is not a mirage. Thank you for preparing us since our human conception for this journey. Free us from our self-inflicted pain and torment; free us from the shackles that we have placed on our own bodies. Free us from idol worship. Humble us that we may be like the 72 followers Your Son chose to demonstrate Your goodness, power, will, and grace. Humble us that we may be devoted stewards loving and honoring You with our heart, mind, body, and soul. In Your Son Jesus' name, I pray. Amen.

SPEAK YOUR TRUTH

Say the words below and write beside them your truth. You can also use the workbook to write your responses.

I Feel...
I Am...
I Believe...
I Am Grateful For...
I Will Improve...
I Am Proud of Myself Because...
I Will Stay Out of My/God's Way By...
Today I Will Focus More on...
And Focus Less on...
Today I Will ...

GO DEEPER!
Please refer to **Day 119** in the workbook.

NOTES

Day 120: Inner Turmoil

Why am I so depressed? Why this turmoil within me? Put your hope in God, for I will still praise Him, my Savior and my God.

—Psalms 42:11 HCSB

Stop this very moment and say, "Thank You, Father, for taking care of every issue that is presented." If you are fighting depression, I want you to recite the first paragraph of today's prayer. With intensity. As though your life depends upon it.

PRAYER

Father, I pray that the moments that I feel the walls coming in too close, that I reach out for You. I pray that even in darkness, that I see Your light, smile, and praise Your holy name. I pray that when there doesn't seem to be a solution, I believe enough in You to solve the problem and show me the way through. Right now, everything that is weighing on me, I pray that You will handle them and show me what to do. I know that You never place on me more than I can handle.

Thank You, Father. Thank You, Father. Thank You, Father. Thank You! Father, I pray for my loved ones who struggle with the belief of depression. I pray for those I don't even know, who also struggle with the belief of depression. Touch the hearts of those who are saddened and fearful. Help those that believe they don't have enough trust and faith in You to take care of them. Father touch the hearts of those who see more darkness than light, and those whose hope slips slowly away. Help them to see Your light even in the smallest of areas. Help them to hear and discern Your voice. Help them to see and recognize Your guardian angels who point the way. Lift them up Father to know and trust You. Lift them up to feel Your weight supporting them. So that they can release their fears into Your capable Hands. Help them to say, "Thank You, Father, for taking care of this for me." In Jesus' name, I pray. Amen.

SPEAK YOUR TRUTH
Say the words below and write beside them your truth. You can also use the workbook to write your responses.

> I Feel...
> I Am...
> I Believe...
> I Am Grateful For...
> I Will Improve...
> I Am Proud of Myself Because...
> I Will Stay Out of My/God's Way By...
> Today I Will Focus More on...
> And Focus Less on...
> Today I Will ...

GO DEEPER!
Please refer to **Day 120** in the workbook.

NOTES

Day 121: Be on Guard

He then told them, "Watch out and be on guard against all greed because one's life is not in the abundance of his possessions."

—Luke 12:15 HCSB

There's a lot of drama going on in the world, at your workplace, in your family, in your home, and within many of you. Some folks are fighting the darkness of greed, while others are succumbing to it or drowning in it. Some of you wake up, stroll through your day, and go to sleep with envy in your hearts. Some of you are fixated on revenge. Kicking someone down or standing on their back to elevate yourself gets you no higher than you already were. It's just your perception that's been altered. God has a way of leveling all playing fields if not today trust me it will be one day.

Remember that what goes around always comes back around. Whether you do good or bad, the cycle of life that God has created must always maintain balance and order. What you put out you receive. Doubt brings slow progress. Evil deeds bring negative consequences. Good deeds bring unlimited blessings. God gives us all choices. Each day you must make a choice.

PRAYER

Father, protect me from greedy and envious people. People who are desperate, and those who are so focused on their hurt that all they want to do is hurt others. Father protect me from me. Protect me during those times when I'm overly focused on money and material possessions. And fearful of things that I can't control—but not reliant upon You to resolve my problems.

Father, I pray for the greedy, prideful, arrogant, and tormented. I pray for the sapsuckers who leach off of others and try to sap the Light out of Your children. I pray for the lazy and shiftless. I pray for myself, for any of these characteristics and behaviors that I may show. May I be freed from this vileness. Move them, Father. Move me, Father. Lift up those of us who wade in the waters of pity. Restore us to our greatness, where our confidence is always in You first. I pray for these things today and always, in Jesus' name. Amen.

SPEAK YOUR TRUTH

Say the words below and write beside them your truth. You can also use the workbook to write your responses.

> I Feel...
> I Am...
> I Believe...
> I Am Grateful For...
> I Will Improve...
> I Am Proud of Myself Because...
> I Will Stay Out of My/God's Way By...
> Today I Will Focus More on...
> And Focus Less on...
> Today I Will ...

GO DEEPER!

Please refer to **Day 121** in the workbook.

NOTES

Day 122: We're Never Sure How We're Being Used

The Lord said, "Go over to Straight Street, to the house of Judas. When you get there, ask for a man from Tarsus named Saul. He is praying to me right now. I have shown him a vision of a man named Ananias coming in and laying hands on him so he can see again."

"But Lord," exclaimed Ananias, "I've heard many people talk about the terrible things this man has done to the believers in Jerusalem! And he is authorized by the leading priests to arrest everyone who calls upon your name." But the Lord said, "Go, for Saul is my chosen instrument to take my message to the Gentiles and to kings, as well as to the people of Israel. And I will show him how much he must suffer for my name's sake."

—Acts 9:11-16 NLT

We're never sure whom God has called upon. We're never sure how God is using us and others to help the least of His children and to spread His love and Word. Don't question Him, just obey.

PRAYER

Father use me, direct me, and open my eyes to see. In Jesus' name. Amen.

SPEAK YOUR TRUTH

Say the words below and write beside them your truth. You can also use the workbook to write your responses.

- I Feel...
- I Am...
- I Believe...
- I Am Grateful For...
- I Will Improve...
- I Am Proud of Myself Because...
- I Will Stay Out of My/God's Way By...
- Today I Will Focus More on...
- And Focus Less on...
- Today I Will ...

GO DEEPER!

Please refer to **Day 122** in the workbook.

NOTES

Day 123: Just Share Your Story

After they had evangelized that town and made many disciples, they returned to Lystra, to Iconium, and to Antioch, strengthening the disciples by encouraging them to continue in the faith and by telling them, "It is necessary to pass through many troubles on our way into the kingdom of God."

—Acts 14:21-22 HCSB

Paul, Barnabas, and some of the other disciples knew that there was strength in numbers. They returned to the towns with more disciples so that they could evangelize to more people. And spread the word of God quicker. The growing discipleship also meant that the mission would continue, even if any of them were jailed, stoned, crucified, or killed. The battle would continue. Is that your approach for sharing God's love and Word? Do you openly share your faith with others? Do you let other people know that you are a believer and follower of Christ? Do you testify beyond the church walls about the great things God has done for you? Consider how your life would be different if you did these things consistently.

PRAYER

Father, I know that times will not always be easy. But I am confident that You will never leave me, so I am comforted in knowing that I am never alone in this journey. Mold me in this process. Remove out of me all things not perfect in Your sight and restore me with Your goodness. Strengthen me to walk through and past trouble, and not engage with ignorant people. Fill me with optimism and squeeze out the cynicism within me. Surround me with believers and followers so that I may fellowship, learn, and gain wisdom. Help me to be more committed in my walk. In Jesus' name, I pray. Amen.

SPEAK YOUR TRUTH

Say the words below and write beside them your truth. You can also use the workbook to write your responses.

I Feel…
I Am…
I Believe…
I Am Grateful For…
I Will Improve…
I Am Proud of Myself Because…
I Will Stay Out of My/God's Way By…
Today I Will Focus More on…
And Focus Less on…
Today I Will …

GO DEEPER!

Please refer to **Day 123** in the workbook.

NOTES

Day 124: It's Not You, It's Him

You may say to yourself, 'My power and my own ability have gained this wealth for me,' but remember that the Lord your God gives you the power to gain wealth, in order to confirm His covenant He swore to your fathers, as it is today.

—Deuteronomy 8:17-18 HCSB

It is not you, it is Him. It really is that simple. All that you have and all that you are is because of Him. Praise Him and give thanks.

PRAYER
Father, You are the reason for my talents, gifts, strengths, successes, and blessings. I cannot do anything without You. Thank You for loving me. Thank You, Father.

SPEAK YOUR TRUTH
Say the words below and write beside them your truth. You can also use the workbook to write your responses.

I Feel…
I Am…

I Believe...
I Am Grateful For...
I Will Improve...
I Am Proud of Myself Because...
I Will Stay Out of My/God's Way By...
Today I Will Focus More on...
And Focus Less on...
Today I Will ...

GO DEEPER!

Please refer to **Day 124** in the workbook.

NOTES

GO BEYOND: Month 4

DEEPER STUDY

This section is devoted to deeper study, reflection, and analysis as you end the month and begin your focus on next month.

- Look at your notes from Days 23 and 24. Can you recall those days? Can you recall how you felt, the things that you heard, and said?
- Review your notes from **Go Beyond— Month 2**. What comes to mind? What are your thoughts?

Retrieve your "For God" container and read aloud the messages inside.

Which "For God" messages have been resolved? Which ones are you still waiting patiently for resolution?

Close your eyes and breathe slowly. Inhale through your nose and exhale through your mouth. Continue breathing slowly until your thoughts also slow down. It may take a few minutes, allow the process to unfold, don't rush it. You can sit or lie down. Just make sure that you're in a relaxed position and state of mind. Slowly say these words aloud, *"God show me what You see for me"*. Keep repeating this until a picture begins to form in your mind. It may take longer for you if your mind has a lot of clutter or if you haven't practiced having conversations with God. Ask God, *"What does this mean Father?"*. Continue asking this question, patiently, making sure to listen and look. Things may not make sense right now. It's okay, just keep inquiring.

Ask God the same question in different ways if you need to. When the conversation is interrupted, end the conversation and thank God for the chat. Then remain where you are seated (or lying) and reflect over the experience. Our conversations can be interrupted because of external distractions. Or because we unknowingly engage our internal brake. You may feel emotional, possibly overwhelmed, or just at peace.

Let yourself feel what you feel. Don't try to block or filter what you feel. This is about you connecting with yourself and connecting with God. We're breaking through barriers, we're changing our habits and thinking, and we're pushing to a new level. Don't hold back, you will block your blessings. Take notes, if you can. Either during or after this session. You will review these notes again later. You can also record your session and then take notes from the recording.

NOTES

NEXT STEPS

At the beginning of each month, you take part in an activity that I call Ponder This.

Now that you have had the chance to ask questions, think, reflect, and probably do a little research of your own— let's Consider This...

Consider This: Month 1

If you think that the name Jesus is Hebrew, you are 100 percent incorrect. If you think that the man that was and is called the Son of God, is named Jesus, you are incorrect. If you think that his Hebrew name translates to Jesus, you are once again incorrect. You can thank our friends the Greeks for this. The man that we have known as Jesus our entire lives is actually named Yeshua. This is translated as Joshua. It was a common name during the Era of the Second Temple.[7]

If you're scratching your head and wondering what in the world is going on, or you're ready to toss this book for insulting your beloved Jesus—please read the section on Jesus, in **Seek Him: Workbook 1** that is aligned with this book. There I go into a lengthy explanation about Yeshua, the man commonly known as Jesus.

What I want you to consider here is this—if we are all spiritual beings, and Yeshua is also a spiritual being, then who is the spiritual being named Jesus? I mean, there are plenty of people who are now called Jesus thanks to the lost-in-translation butchering of Yeshua's name. Does it really matter to Yeshua that we call him Jesus? Maybe not. After calling him Jesus for as long as you have, do you feel moved to begin calling him Yeshua? Or do you think that you're just too hard-wired to switch things up? Is it that big of a deal to you? Possibly not. I just wanted to give you an opportunity to consider these things and more.

Consider This: Month 2

Would you be at all surprised to find out that the phrase, "*This too shall pass*" is not from or in the Bible? It is actually an old Persian adage that was translated and used in multiple languages. This phrase is thought to have originated through the writings of medieval Persian Sufi poets such as Rumi.[8] In case you didn't know, Persian, also known as Farsi, is a Western Iranian language. The phrase and fable have even been used in Jewish folklore.[9]

So how in the world did it seemingly become a Western world phrase? Well, thanks to a 19th-century retelling of a Persian fable by the English poet Edward FitzGerald, it became popular. Even President Abraham Lincoln is quoted retelling the fable in 1859.[10] Interesting, isn't it? If you have been reciting this phrase thinking that you recall it from the Bible, now you know the truth.

Consider This: Month 3

Did you read and do the activity in the **Ponder This** section for Month 3? Most of us were probably shocked to hear and read these words written by Matthew as an account of Jesus's sermon. We probably assumed that Matthew heard Jesus wrong. Or that Jesus was setting the bar too high for us to reach. Who wants to voluntarily be slapped for a second time? Who is going to give more in a lawsuit than what they have to? Why would we walk the extra mile if we were already forced to walk a mile against our wishes?

I have to thank Kerric, for sharing an analysis from Shane Willard.[11] Shane is a pastor who is mentored by another pastor with rabbinical training. He teaches the context of the Scriptures from a Hebraic perspective. From time to time I listen to Shane's recorded messages. I love how he uses historical, religious, political, legal, and cultural perspectives to help provide people with a better understanding of why, how, and where things were done, and by whom. Shane explained in great detail this part of Jesus's sermon. Once you hear it, it makes complete sense once you know the background information. I also did my independent research to confirm what was shared. Let's look at the verses again and I will separate them. Then I will provide the analysis and what we could see as Jesus's perspective:

"You have heard that it was said, 'AN EYE FOR AN EYE, AND A TOOTH FOR A TOOTH." I learned from my reading and studying the Bible, that you have to pay close attention to the words being used and how they

are being used. Most people focus on the part where Jesus says, "*An eye for an eye, and a tooth for a tooth,*" but you are missing the one word before all of that, which is "said". Jesus was not changing the meaning, he was clarifying a misconception. He did not say, "*As it was written*", he said, "*You have heard that it was said*", which means that it was not written scripture.[12] The common misconception seems to be that people were using Exodus 21:24–25 (the guidelines for a magistrate to punish convicted offenders) as a justification for personal vengeance. However, Jesus was clearing things up and letting them know that basically, "*You heard it but it isn't God's law*".

Are you ready to tackle Jesus's next statement that followed the eye for an eye, tooth for tooth comment? "*... do not resist an evil person; but whoever slaps you on your right cheek, turn the other to him also*". In his book, *Engaging the Powers: Discernment and Resistance in a World of Domination,*[13] Walter Wink wrote that when a person hit another person that they deemed beneath them, they would do so with the back of their left hand. It was a way of asserting dominance and authority. It demeaned the person being slapped. Why? Traditional Jewish and Muslim people eat with their right hand and when they go to the restroom, they use their left hand. The left hand, for many traditionalists, is considered unclean. Imagine being slapped with the hand that someone uses to wipe their buttocks. So then why in the world would Jesus tell people to accept the slap and turn the other cheek for it to also be slapped?

Jesus knew that the moment you turn the other cheek, the person who slapped you is now faced with a dilemma. An alternative would be that the slapper could use the palm of their hand and slap you, or they could punch you. However, if they did this then that would mean that the person they were slapping or hitting was their equal. And not beneath them. As the backhanded left-hand slap would declare. By turning the other cheek, you are demanding equality. You are telling the person who slapped you that you are not beneath them, you are their equal. Jesus also knew that the only way to slap my left cheek is if you use your right hand, the same hand that you eat with. The hand that is to never be "unclean". They would not even consider taking that swing. So it becomes a stare-off.

Imagine that. Someone backhands you and you turn the other cheek and stare at them with a smirk or glare on your face. Without saying a word, you're saying, *"Yeah, now let's do this as equals. I double dare you!"* Jesus was empowering people. He was teaching them how to stand up for themselves without having to be violent, act a fool, or break the law. I don't know about you, but I can't help but laugh at the thought of people learning this practice and walking around turning the other cheek. At some point, you know that traditionalists slowed down on the backhanded slap. I wonder if that is why people switched 1,500 years later to slapping people with gloves, as the first step in challenging someone to a duel. So now that you know the historical and cultural perspectives, can you see why Jesus said to turn the other cheek?

Are you ready to examine the other two statements that Jesus made that day? "*...If anyone wants to sue you and take your shirt, let him have your coat also....*" This statement could leave you scratching your head unless you understand the historical, legal, and cultural context of that time. If you owed someone money and they came to collect and they took your shirt. This was forbidden by Hebrew law as stated in Deuteronomy (24:10–13). If you then go a step farther and hand over your coat (cloak) that would mean that you were standing there naked. Public nakedness brought shame to not just the naked person but to every person who saw your naked body. Walter Wink's book also points to Noah's case (Genesis 9:20–23). So can you see Jesus's mindset?

If you want to take the shirt off of my back and humiliate me, then I'm going to shame you in the process by stripping naked. Let's walk in this shame together, and everyone who sees my nakedness also carries the shame. I can see how this helps to enforce in the laws the recovery limits in lawsuits. You can't leave someone "naked". Great strategy Jesus! Now let's look at the third statement: "*...Whoever forces you to go one mile, go with him two...*" The Romans had a law called the Angaria,[14] which their government adopted from the Persians. It was like a postal system. The Persian system was enacted by their king, Cyrus the Great (which we will discuss later in this book). Roman couriers on horseback would be stationed at different points along the roads and they would transmit messages from the government. One courier would ride and meet up with another courier and hand off the message to the next courier until it ultimately reached its destination. The term Angaria eventually took on the meaning of any compulsory service of animals or humans. The law allowed the Roman authorities to demand that residents of occupied territories carry messages and equipment the distance of one-mile post. But the law prohibited forcing an individual to go farther than a single mile, at the risk of suffering disciplinary actions. The disciplinary actions could be a loss of wages for the day.

Since the Romans had occupied the Jewish lands, they could then demand a resident to carry messages and equipment for them. Knowing this and knowing that the Angaria law was unjust and demeaning, Jesus instructed people to go beyond the one mile they were ordered to walk. He said to walk two miles. Jesus knew that by walking the extra mile, the Roman couriers would be punished for violating the law. He also assumed rightly, that the couriers would eventually grow tired of being disciplined and stop forcing the residents to do the work that the couriers were supposed to do. Absolutely genius on the part of Jesus.

QUESTIONS

1. What are your thoughts about this?
2. Have your opinions changed from earlier? In what ways?
3. What did you learn that you did not already know?

Consider This: Month 4

Hopefully, you did not cheat and flip quickly to this page before completing the **Ponder This** section at the beginning of **Month 4**. Let's see if your answers align with the information that I have provided here. As you may know, the Bible has been misinterpreted and mistranslated. With this confusion, there is also confusion over who makes up the Jews, Gentiles, Greeks, Proselytes, Hellenists, Nations, and Strangers, that the Bible mentions.

Greeks, Jews, and Hellenists

Let's start with the Greeks, Jews, and Hellenists. About 150 years before the New Testament the Greeks conquered the land of Israel and forced the Jews to surrender their national heritage, culture, and their beloved Torah. They were forced to adopt Greek culture, language, and religion. Some Jews adopted the Greek way of life and chose to reject the Torah. They were called Hellenes or Hellenists. Other Jews who despised all-things Greek, revolted and killed both Greeks and Hellenists. The divide between traditional Jews and Hellenes continued through the first century A.D. When you read the word Hellenes in the New Testament, it is translated as "Greek" but also as "Gentile", but never in the context of native Greeks, but rather the Jews that chose to adopt the Greek culture and language.

Gentiles and Nations

You probably already have your chest puffed out with the answer as to what a nation is and who makes up a nation. So let me ask you, who are the gentiles? Many of you probably answered, "non-Jews", and you would be wrong. The words "ethnos" and "goy" are translated to mean "nation". Things got tricky when the Greek word "ethnos" in the New Testament was translated to mean "gentile". The word gentile means "one belongs to a tribe or clan". A nation is any group of people working and living under one rule. Examples of nations include Israel, Egyptians, Canaanites, Arameans, Moabites, etc.

Do you recall in Genesis 12:2 when God said he would make Israel a great nation? The ten lost tribes from the northern "nation" of Israel are the ethnon (plural of ethnos). They make up the Nations. In the Book of Acts, when Paul preached to the "nations", he was preaching to the ten lost tribes. By the way, they weren't actually lost, like in the literal sense. They weren't missing. People knew where they were. They were spiritually lost, disconnected from God's teachings and principles. Just like when we tell someone "You have lost your mind". When James mentioned being a servant of the twelve tribes, he was including in that number the ten "lost" tribes. There you go, some bonus content for you!

Proselytes and Strangers

Did you search online to answer my question about Proselytes? Or did you give it your best shot and answer what you thought to be the correct answer? Hopefully, you did the latter. But I can understand if you rushed over to your favorite search engine. The word Proselytes is a Greek transliteration, which means "foreigner" or "stranger". It is mentioned four times in the New Testament (Matthew 23:15, Acts 2:11, 6:5, and 13:43). In some translations, you will see they used the word "convert" instead of a proselyte. So be sure to check more than one version, if you only see the word "convert". Proselytes are non-Jews (non-Israelites) who joined Israel and followed God's teachings. They converted to Judaism. Which means, basically, many of you have been calling non-Jews "gentiles" when you were supposed to be calling them Proselytes. Let's see if you can make that verbal switch moving forward. If you recall, there were always foreigners and strangers that lived amongst the Israelites. In the book of Exodus, when Israel left Egypt, others joined them. In the book of Leviticus, God told the Israelites that the same laws that applied to them applied to the foreigner that lived with them. They were to be accepted and treated as any other Israelite.

Well, there you go!

Did you learn something new? Did you say, "That can't be true," and begin searching online? I hope the answers to both questions was "yes". You should always seek answers to your questions, confirm people's statements, and do your independent research. It keeps you from getting caught up in the web of the grapevine. I hope this piques your interest in exploring more facts and truth of the Bible and the eras and people it memorializes. I have more Ponder This and Consider This trivia to share with you in **Seek Him, Volume 2: Going Beyond Your Spiritual Comfort Zone**. If you have not purchased your copy yet, don't delay, you don't want to miss out on the next four months of this awesome journey!

Conclusion

This marks the end of this book. Thank you for joining me on this four-month journey. I hope that the past 124 days have helped you to feel more comfortable seeking God through all things, not just during tough times. I hope that you have learned more about yourself and the things that motivate you and paralyze you. Each month you took baby steps towards greater progress in your life.

I hope that you found **Seek Him: Workbook 1** as an added benefit. If you did not purchase it, consider doing so. Next year, you can pick up both of these books, and beginning on Day 1, you can track your growth and development in comparison to where you are this year. The workbook is for everyone who wants a greater challenge.

You now have the option of repeating this book, until you feel like you have truly tested your spiritual comfort zone. Or, if you think you're ready, you can start the next phase of this journey by reading **Seek Him, Volume 2: Going Beyond Your Spiritual Comfort Zone**. It covers four more months of prayers, reflections, affirmations, and lessons. **Seek Him: Workbook 2** is its companion workbook. You can purchase both books online or through your local book retailers. Information on all three can be found at the end of this book. I will see you on the next leg of our journey!

—Natasha

NOTES

PONDER THIS: MONTH 1

[1] ^ Spiritual beings in human form: Please read more about this in the **Seek Him: Workbook 1**

DAY 1

[2] ^ Oxford Languages. Retrieved from http://english.oxforddictionaries.com/virtuous

[3] ^ Dictionary.com Retrieved from https://www.dictionary.com/browse/virtuous

DAY 20

[4] ^ The "liar" is another name for the devil, satan, the "enemy", and lucifer.

PONDER THIS: MONTH 3

[5] ^ Matthew 5:38-41 NASB

DAY 102

[6] ^ Joel Osteen. Pastor, Lakewood Church. Joel Osteen Ministries. JoelOsteen.com

CONSIDER THIS: MONTH 1

[7] ^ Second Temple period has disputed dates from 516 BCE and 70 CE compared to 352 BCE to 68 CE. The first set of dates were outlined in Richard Parker & Waldo Dubberstein's Babylonian Chronology, 626 B.C.–A.D. 75, Brown University

Press: Providence 1956, p. 30. The second set of dates come from Maimonides' Questions & Responsa, responsum # 389, Jerusalem 1960 (Hebrew).

CONSIDER THIS: MONTH 2

[8] ^ Keyes, Ralph (2006). The quote Verifier: Who Said What, Where, and When. Macmillan. pp. 159–160. ISBN 0-312-34004-4.

[9] ^ Leiman, Shnayer Z. (Spring 2008). "Judith Ish-Kishor: This Too Shall Pass". Tradition: A Journal of Orthodox Jewish Thought. 41 (1): 71–77. JSTOR 23263507

[10] ^ "Address before the Wisconsin State Agricultural Society". Abraham Lincoln Online. Milwaukee, Wisconsin. September 30, 1859.

CONSIDER THIS: MONTH 3

[11] ^ Shane Willard Ministries (November 28, 2016). The Sermon on the Mount. Retrieved from https://vimeo.com/ondemand/86914/193477920

[12] ^ Avi-Yonah, Michael. The Jews Under Roman and Byzantine Rule: A Political History of Palestine from the Bar Kokhba War to the Arab Conquest.

[13] ^ Wink, Walter (1992). Engaging the Powers: Discernment and Resistance in a World of Domination. Fortress Press. pp. 175–82. ISBN 978-0-80062646-4.

[14] ^ "Angaria", Encyclopædia Britannica, 2 (9th ed.), 1878, p. 26

MORE THANK YOU'S

I want to thank some individuals who although did not help me with the creation of this book, did however help in other ways that I want to acknowledge.

To my Dad, although you're no longer here in the physical sense, you're always here. You helped to root me in my spiritual and religious beliefs. You taught me how to pray, connect, heal, embrace healing, and to be a critical thinker. You inspired and encouraged my writing since childhood. I pursued journalism because of you. I type each word in my blogs and my books thinking of you. Thank you. I love and miss you!

I want to thank my grandparents, who are no longer here in the physical sense. My paternal great-grandmother, Georgia Lee Newton. My paternal grandmother Dorrisene N. Foreman. They inspired me through their religious faith, conviction, teaching, healing, and writings. Their published works helped me to refocus and remain committed. Thank you to my maternal grandmother, Maxine B. Stephens. She was a dedicated and tenacious woman, a servant leader, a woman whose love for God flowed into her love for His children. I did not finish writing this book before my grandmothers transitioned, but I know they are still proud of me.

I would like to thank my grandfathers, Robert Foreman, Sr. and Elisberry Stephens, and my great-grandfather H.C. Butler. These men showed me love, strength, courage, honor, and discipline. I pray to continue to honor my grandparents' legacies.

Thank you to my cousins Princess Peoples and Damion Wallace, for your loving support and checking in on my progress. To other family members who have cheered for me through text messages and social media, thank you. I love you all! I also thank my Breaking Bread family; to those of you who have walked with me along this journey from the very beginning, and to those of you who have recently connected with me through my blog or social media. I look forward to this continued journey together. Juanita Bryan, Lavonya Jones, Eboni Brown, and Sandy Poag thank you for encouraging me to write this book and supporting me through the process. I hope to gain your feedback as advanced readers for my next books.

To Shasta Moore, thank you for being my prayer partner for several years, and for checking up on me when I come to mind. Some of the things that you taught and shared with me inspired some of my writing. Thank you, Kenya Ware, for forwarding me daily devotionals via text message in 2008. You helped to spark one of the flames inside of me, to reflect and pray in a way that I hadn't done before. I turned my reflections and prayers into my blog. That effort has led me to this book.

Thank you to De'Leice Drane. You encouraged me to run towards God and stop running away from my purpose and destiny. You explained that daily we walk in ministry. Thank you for helping me to see and embrace this. The next person that I would like to thank is probably the one that most people would not expect for me to mention—because that is what we do when we're being immature and petty. I want to thank my ex-husband, John Hope Bryant. August 2016 you sat next to me as I began mapping out this book. I didn't know then what would come from my effort. You encouraged me and although God's vision for my writing is much broader, deeper, and bolder than what you thought this would be, I still thank you for your initial support years ago.

I thank SirJames Buchanon. You were always more than an assistant. You were and are my friend. I'm grateful that God placed you in my life, exactly when you were needed. Thank you for your counsel and for even admitting when your honorable intentions got undesirable results. Thank you for sharing your story, your truth, and your authentic self. Thank you for the laughs and for letting me go off on you countless times in 2017. Only you, God, and I know what that means!

I would like to thank Dr. Bernice A. King, Rev. Raphael G. Warnock, and Ambassador Andrew Young. All three of you shared candid stories with me about your personal and spiritual journeys. You shared the struggles and fears that come from standing tall in your convictions. Thank you for being transparent and for encouraging me to go where God guides me.

I started with Elohim, and I end this with Elohim, so together we can continue this journey to what's next!

About the Author

Natasha L. Foreman is an entrepreneur, college professor, author, and podcaster. A Southern California native, Natasha now resides in Atlanta, Georgia with her Labrador Retriever, Bishop Milo Bryant. Since 2009, she has been sharing her spiritual journey and God's love through her blog, Breaking Bread With Natasha. She is a self-proclaimed servant leader, who boldly shares her stories, testimonies, and love for her Creator. This, from a person who spent years in the "closet" about her religious and spiritual beliefs.

When she's not working, Natasha enjoys reading books, playing cards, and video games, hiking, traveling, listening and dancing to music (especially from the 1970s and 1980s), and spending quality time with loved ones. She's also a foodie, who enjoys cooking and sampling cuisine from around the world. So yes, you can break bread with her— spiritually and literally.

Connect with Natasha through any of these sources:
http://twitter.com/breakbread365
http://facebook.com/breakingbreadwithnatasha
http://natashaforeman.com
http://breakingbreadwithnatasha.com

Sign up for our newsletter to stay in the loop about our newest book releases, events, and more: http://domelifepublishing.com

Visit DOMELifePublishing.com for more details about these and other books by Natasha:

SEEK HIM: WORKBOOK 1

Use this workbook with Seek Him, Volume 1. It encourages readers to dig deeper and consider where you currently are compared to where you want to be in your life and in your relationships with God and others. It provides greater context into historical, cultural, and social norms to further assist you.

SEEK HIM, VOLUME 2: GOING BEYOND YOUR SPIRITUAL COMFORT ZONE

This book picks up where Seek Him, Volume 1 leaves off. Another four months of exploration, reflection, questions, and pushing yourself beyond your spiritual comfort zone. The book intensifies to align with your expected growth over time.

SEEK HIM: WORKBOOK 2

This workbook addresses the themes and correlating daily messages in Seek Him, Volume 2: Going Beyond Your Spiritual Comfort Zone. Just like in Workbook 1, you will go deeper into your exploration of the Bible and your relationships with God, self, and others. You are challenged and encouraged to apply in real-time what you are learning and revealing through your daily walk.